Financial Freedom by Faith

Roxanne Simone Lord

Copyright © 2016 Roxanne Simone Lord

All rights reserved.

ISBN-13:
978-0692823392 (Ican Ministries Network)

ISBN-10:
0692823395

DEDICATION

To my best friend, my angel investor, my backer, the wind beneath my wings, Jesus

TABLE OF CONTENTS

1. What is Money? — 3
2. Manifesting Money. — 12
3. Wealthy by Nature — 28
4. Show Me the Money — 39
5. The Plans of the Diligent … — 51
6. Where There is a Will….. — 64
7. Bootstrapper Extraordinaire — 72
8. Restoring the Broken — 79
9. The Power of Faith — 92
10. Faith versus Money — 102
11. Ways to Make Money — 117
12. The Harvest — 132
13. Blood Red Tomatoes — 140
14. Becoming a Millionaire — 146
15. How to Make Millions by Faith — 156
16. Plan for Prosperity — 162
17. Anointed to Lead — 178
18. Paralysis — 187

TABLE OF CONTENTS
(Continued)

19. Wisdom — 204

20. Promotion — 213

Financial Freedom by Faith

ACKNOWLEDGMENTS

I would like to acknowledge my husband Martin Marcelle for encouraging me and standing by me to fulfil my purpose. To my family, the Holy Ghost Upper Room by Faith Tabernacle, community and friends, thank you for uplifting me. To my friend Bishop Michael Jones and all who have shaped my destiny, thank you and may God continue to bless and keep you.

1

What Is Money?

Money is a tool designed to represent the value of something. That value is set by supply and demand of the item or service and is based on what the people are willing to pay for it.

According to Wikipedia: "Money is any item or verifiable record that is **generally accepted as payment for goods and services and repayment of debts in a particular country.**"

People fall in love with money because of the type of life it can afford them. With money you can buy a lot of goods and services, as many as you like, wherever you like. Without money you feel stuck in places, homes and neighborhoods you don't necessarily like. Without money you eat what you can afford, mostly at home, because if you don't have money you cannot dine out at fine restaurants or go out to plays and be entertained.

The standard of life for people with money and for people without money are vastly different. We can change this with a little product called faith. Faith is not something that one can patent or copyright. It is something however that can level the playing field between the rich and the poor.

The very first step in eradicating lack and poverty from your life is to understand what money is and stop believing that you are poor. Money as dollars and cents, pounds and yen did not always exist. First we had a barter system. Augusto Graziani, an Italian Professor of Economics, asked this question," How does a monetary economy differ from one in which trade occurs by barter?"

The answer is that in a monetary economy, like the one we live in today, a tool was skillfully invented to value goods and services. So we no longer have to walk around with cows and goats or even gold bars to pay for things we need or desire. Since money is, in effect, a "social contrivance" something cheaply created for convenience sake, then it follows that money in itself is valueless, it's just a piece of paper, but the goods or services behind the money carry real value.

It follows then, that for you to create wealth or even to get money you must have goods or services. The more in demand your goods and services are, the more people will want them and exchange money to you to pay for those goods and services. What goods, products, art or services can you provide to the world? What are your gifts or talents? What do you love doing or can do extraordinarily well? What's your passion?

Many people today have similar goods and services to what you have to offer. For you to command attention and gain more money than your competitor, you must have an edge. You must have a plan or strategy to stand out from the crowd. I say to you today that faith can be an edge. Faith is simply the boldness to take an action that can change your situation or your life. Most times faith carries great risk. For instance, Abraham's faith was tested when God asked him to sacrifice his only son. He heard that little still voice and he did not back out or pretend he didn't hear God's voice. Instead he moved obediently to do what he heard God speak to his spirit.

God will always send the provision when He gives you a vision. In Abraham's case, God sent a ram in the bushes and Abraham was able to unloose his only son Isaac from the sacrifice table. And God blessed Abraham bountifully. Whenever you obey God, He blesses you abundantly. There is a passage that I have come to love. Psalm 28:7, "The Lord is my strength and my shield, my heart trusteth in the Lord and I am helped, therefore, my soul will always rejoice in the Lord."

In Hebrews, the quintessential book of faith, it starts off with a description of faith. "Now faith is the substance of things hoped for, the evidence of things not seen." Hebrews 11.1

Many people don't understand this because it is lofty. Simply put, "Faith is confidence that God will make a way out of no way." For people who feel they have nothing, I want to introduce this valuable substance called faith. It works like currency to me and is much more valuable than currency because it is based on trusting the Almighty Creator rather than the government or bank.

Money is pretty much a glorified promissory note. Currency is a system of exchange backed by man-made banks and government. Faith was invented before money or currency, is backed by God himself, you can use faith in any country and it's weightless, so much easier to carry around. It is also thief-proof in many instances. I say many instances because many people allow others to steal their faith by stealing their confidence. Too many people get broke in spirit which is often followed by being broke financially.

Divorce breaks up families and breaks hearts and spirits

too. Satan is clever to know what will destroy a man or woman in the physical, emotional and spiritual realm. Divorce messes people up financially. It messes up the children too much more than people know. Divorce can break a man's spirit. Many times he or she does not even realize how destructive the divorce was to their spirit, self-esteem and faith. People jump into new relationships carrying all their old baggage, old unhealed wounds into the new. Investing in books and seminars on self-development, financial development and spiritual development feed and repair the mind and soul. They also help to rejuvenate and reinvent broken lives and broken spirits.

People tend to ignore faith until they have lost all their wealth. Then when they are down and out, have few friends and no job, they get a chance to wonder what they've been doing with their lives.

What if we were taught how to use our faith from day one, consider how wealthy and healthy we would become. We would trust God to send the right spouse, we would not settle for less because of fear of getting old. We would take some calculated risks, open businesses, buy property and live our dreams if we knew that we were backed fully by God.

Many have put their trust in money, government and banks and not in God. Although it says on the dollar bill, In God We Trust. God is the highest authority. When we go straight to God and stay focused on God, we will be wealthy. "I will lift up mine eyes unto the hills, from whence cometh my help." (Psalm 121.1)

Real wealth comes from thoughts, ideas, action, discernment, wisdom, faith, courage, persistence and determination. How do you get all of the above? By praying, meditating, listening and obeying God who sends the Holy Spirit to guide you, counsel you and strengthen you. "Remember the Lord thy God for it is He that gives you power to get wealth." Deuteronomy 8:18

When you put God first all things that you desire follow you. How does this work?

Remember that God created the world in six days by first thought then words. He spoke the word and it was. You are made in God's image. You are his creations. You are an heir to the throne of righteousness, you are His righteousness. He gave you power to create. Power to manifest whatever your heart's desires.

2

Manifesting Money

In the beginning God created the earth from a thought, he then spoke the earth into existence. He made the sun, the moon and the stars. He created man and woman from nothing. And He blessed them and said these words to the man and woman he created from dirt.

"Be fruitful, and multiply, and replenish the earth, and subdue it: and have dominion over the fish of the sea, and over the fowl of the air, and over every living thing that moveth upon the earth." Genesis 1:28

Now let's fast forward, here some of us are. Some have no money, no wealth, no home, no car, no job, some have no family and some have no one to love.

It's easy to get depressed when you believe that you have nothing. But look again. You have much more than you think. And do you have any dirt? Look at what God, our creator did with a bit of dirt. He created life. And consider that you are made in His image. As long as you have life and a working brain, you have hope.

You can dream up a reality for yourself and go about creating it with a plan.

So you have no money. God didn't either. He used thoughts, words and actions. Your thoughts, words and actions will create your wealth or your poverty. It's your decision. So you see wealth begins inside and it is a choice. So too are happiness and joy.

You can choose to see yourself as wealthy or you can continue to see yourself as poor and without.

As long as you believe you are rich, these thoughts will lead to ideas to a plan which will find a way to manifest outwardly. That's faith in action. You will say to the mountain, move and it shall move. Your faith attracts God's blessings. (Which He already gave to you in Genesis 1:28, when you were created.) The greater the faith, the greater the blessings. You serve a great God.

So dream up big dreams, think big ideas. Donald Trump said you are going to be thinking anyway, why not think big.

God is waiting for you to move, when you move, He moves. I have found great favor in volunteering. Things happen when you step out and volunteer. You meet people who are doing something big and you help them, their grace and favor falls on you, you get blessed. So it's not always about finding and accepting a great job. It is certainly awesome when you are looking for a job and find a great one, but to you who cannot find a job, maybe you are considered too old, too whatever, maybe you don't have an employee mentality. To you, there are endless other possibilities. It's about what you have to offer to the world.

Money is worthless paper. It was invented to be a means of exchange and a storage of wealth. If we went back to the barter system, would you be wealthy or poor? You would take your stuff to exchange for what you need. Each person has a gift, something to exchange, that's how you conducted barter. You brought whatever you had out to the market or world, and you got what you needed from the other person.

So what is your gift? What can you do or make to exchange for the things you need? If you are unable to make anything, or if you are not making anything, you will be poor. Same situation with money. If you can't or are not making or doing something that people need or want, you will be poor.

Your product and service must then be taken outside of your home to the world. Unless you have a store or set up shop in your home they won't come to get it. So you have to go out into the world and tell them, show them what you have. For example, Beyoncé has great wealth. She uses her gift, she sings for a living. She is also a great entertainer. People all over the world like looking at her. She has packaged her service well and is marketing well. People like her gifts and they pay for her CDs. Take Donald Trump, our President Elect at this time. He started off in real estate. He had a rich dad. So do you. He started off with a one million loan from his dad. You need a plan to take to your rich Abba (Hebrew for daddy) Proverbs 21:5 says," The plans of the diligent surely lead to profit; and everyone who is hasty surely rushes to poverty."

What do you have home that you can start with? Maybe you only have dirt, but look at what God made with dirt? Civilization. Start living the life you are meant to live. Don't wait. Start living today. You will need the following:

1. Ideas, Vision
2. Pen and Paper to write down the ideas, write down the vision
3. Pray for a strategic plan as you do the research and development of your idea.

4. Courage. What if you fail? Failing brings you closer to victory. Failure will teach you how to do things better next time. It shows you the pitfalls.
5. Faith. You will need faith to step out on a limb.
6. Prepare to Act. Time to make your move using all of the above. Jump. God will send a parachute if you have prepared well.
7. You will need determination and persistence, what if the people don't want to buy what you're selling? Someone will buy, keep going, and don't stop selling.
8. Be patient. Some businesses take some time to take off. The world is now hearing about you and your product or services. Rome was not built in one day.

9. You will need wisdom and discernment to tweak your plan, product or services to meet the needs of the public.

10. Take Jesus as your business partner, he said, "You can do all things through Christ who strengthens you." (Phil 4:13)

I always believed I would be rich. As a young girl, I used to dream of flying. My dreams were so realistic that I would wake up in the morning and flap my arms, concentrate deeply and try to lift off. My feet never left the ground, but in my dreams, they would leave and I would go high up so easily so effortlessly, it was the simplest thing in the world. I never could understand why my body would not obey my mind like in my dreams. So I kept trying, with my eyes closed, I would whisper lift off and command my feet to leave the ground and take me upward. Eventually I gave up. I started to believe that maybe my dreams of flying were more psychological than realistic.

I choose to believe that my dreams meant that I would be a star. I started to believe that God had great plans for my life and that to me explained my dream of flying so effortlessly. Some part of me wondered if I was a witch, because these flying dreams continued until I was well into my thirties. I remembered Joseph's dreams found in Genesis 37:5. "Joseph had a dream, and when he told it to his brothers, they hated him all the more. He said to them, "Listen to this dream I had: [7]We were binding sheaves of grain out in the field when suddenly my sheaf rose and stood upright, while your sheaves gathered around mine and bowed down to it."

I used to tell my sisters my dreams and they hated me for having those dreams. I was also an honor student while they struggled with maintaining passing grades. I was a bookworm, I still love reading. My auntie gave me my first book and kept feeding me books when she realized that I loved reading.

All of this shaped me to believe that I was going to be a very wealthy lady someday. I was born to poor parents but I felt rich and special as a child. As I grew into teenage years, my family structure changed drastically. My mother migrated to the USA and I was left with my dad and my sister. By that time, I was attending one of the most prestigious schools in Trinidad, Bishop Anstey High School. My family did not want to yank me away from such an academically successful school to send me to public high school in Brooklyn, New York. They decided that I should stay and finish school and so I stayed and my sister who was going to a junior secondary school that was not well known for its academics was sent to the USA to live with my mom.

I was lonely and heartbroken, especially since my dad worked nights. My teenage years were horrible. I did manage to graduate high school and I left Trinidad and came to live in America.

My dad was not much of a businessman at all but he had a college education and had a government job. My mother on the other hand, had no education but she was a business woman. She always had something to sell and she always found a market for her products and services. She had ideas, she had plans, she always prayed and she had courage to manifest those ideas with a plan. My mom always wanted to make something of herself and she did her best for her children. She was a great cook and she started a business cooking for the "Yankee sailors". When the sailors left, she used to make 100 pies daily and send me to deliver them to a store who would pay me $50 for the pies. I would ride my bike to take those little pies. The store owner sold them for $1 each.

My mom also made "polorri' and "roti" which she put in a glass display case and every evening we would all go to the park next to us and she would set up a mobile shop. Everyone enjoyed these snacks and she would sell out by the time we went inside.

So suffice it to say, by the time my mom left Trinidad, although she was not there for me in my teenage years, she had taught me how to make money.

In America, I went on to get a college degree. It was hard for me because my parents were not able to fund my education. Thank God for Pell and Tap grants. I had to pay rent though and those grants were not enough to cover my expenses. For a while I had to go on welfare, as a full time student, but I invested the welfare money and started a business.

My mom did show me how to sew. So I started a business called Mind, Body & Soul Inc. I sewed curtains for people's bedrooms, kitchen, shower, living room, dining room, sun room, whatever room you wanted a new look, a creative, regal look, I came in and transformed those rooms. My fame grew and I got a lot of customers. I was able to take myself through college while supporting myself and my two children as a single mom. I graduated, got a great job, eventually got married to a preacher man that changed my entire life and put me on a new road. I can't say that I never looked back at my old life, because I did and I suffered for looking back. I didn't turn into a pillar of salt but looking back, aka, backsliding was part of my life for a long time. God was still working on me, I was being processed and pruned for the kingdom work.

The peculiar thing is that when you are searching for God, He finds you. I was looking for enlightenment, I wanted a better life for me and my children. I met a preacher man twice my age and I found salvation. He was walking with God, so when I met Him, I was introduced to God in a very personal way.

When I met the reverend, he was not employed. I asked him how he survived, he told me that God took care of him. His exact words were, "My God shall supply all my needs according to His riches and glory through Christ Jesus." (Phil 4:19. I thought he was being lofty but then I realized he was speaking the truth. The man had no congregation left, except one lady, yet he had food, he had riches, he had water, he had shelter.

He convinced me to marry him. He said, "God wants a marriage between us." I said, "No way, you're too old for me." He said, "You'll see, you will do as God wants,

His will shall be done." Six months later, I was married to him. He taught me about ministry, he taught me about God. I was a bad pupil, always rebelling. I was ashamed about the age difference between us, he looked like grandpa, a handsome grandpa, but grandpa nonetheless. I loved him, but not in the way he wanted me too. It was a spiritual marriage and I didn't know what that was. My search results came up nothing at the library. Google was just a start up at that time whose door I would knock on looking for business. I worked at a major shipping company at the time and Google had nothing to ship.

So I wrote a book on what a spiritual marriage is. It was my first book, called the Last Castle in Brooklyn. Our 'spiritual marriage' was a disaster, the age difference being the culprit. I am saying all this to you to let you know that God will use you where you are. You don't have to be perfect to come to God. He is the Creator, the master, He will iron out all your imperfections as you press forward towards the prize, which is your highest calling, which is you reaching your highest potential through Christ Jesus.

Reverend said that God would mold me into who He wanted me to become. He said I was being molded to take over his ministry, that I was going to be his successor. He said that I was going to do a great job and grow the ministry from that one last member to a worldwide ministry. When he died in 2006, I was so sorry for not being a better wife to him, the kind he had wanted me to be. But his training remained in me. I took over the ministry and I took God as my partner just as he had done. Armed with little except knowledge, courage, determination and the love of God, I continued the reverend's legacy.

3

Wealthy by Nature

In order to be wealthy you have to first start believing yourself wealthy. "Be ye transformed by the renewing of your mind." Romans 12. You must start thinking new thoughts by feeding yourself new information. If you are hanging around poor people with the wrong mentality then you will not be feeding your mind any new thoughts. You must separate yourself from 'the same ole' stuff daily. You can get new friends by simply hanging out in new places. Libraries not near your home. Try the library in the big city for example. There are business sections to the library, pick up the New York Times, the Wall Street Journal, see what's going on with wealthy folks. Read what they read. Go places where they hang out. Join Meet Up groups, there are so many Meet Ups, but I love the Inventors' Meet Ups. Those are spectacular, filled with people who are inventing things. Most are free or have a nominal charge. There are film meet ups, dance and yoga meet ups, meet ups for people who want to eat differently and change their life by changing their diet.

Many diseases such as diabetes and cancer are linked to diet. You are what you eat. Some of these diseases boil down to your choices. Most diseases are chosen by you, your habits and your lifestyle. You can choose to eat the recommended three servings of vegetables such as kale, broccoli, parsley and asparagus daily or you can choose to consume French fries, white bread, white sugar, cake, ice cream, pork, shrimp, lobster, lots of red meat daily. You choose what disease attaches to your body by what you choose to eat and how you choose to consume it. Juicing is very beneficial to your body. We can choose to juice our vegetables daily or we can choose to continue cooking the vitamins out of them, especially by zapping all those very essential enzymes and nutrients by microwaving our food. Again, being transformed by the renewing of your mind means that you can change your health for better health. You can change habits and lifestyle for a better quality of life.

You can change your financial status also by what you know, learn and practice. The first step is see yourself successful and develop a plan to get there. The objection here is often money to start or capital. Some people don't believe that they have anything. They are miserable because they perceive that they have nothing. Everyone was given something. You have more than you know. Your eyes might see nothing but look again, look deeper this time. What talents and gifts did God give you? It's time to unearth them. It's time to bring the gold, your wealth out of you. So get ready to start digging deeper into your mind.

Your mind is fertile. Especially if you have been feeding it rich nutrients and vitamins. The human brain is like rich fertile soil. You feed it, nourish it with good food and lots of water, the human brain is made up of approximately seventy five percent of water. The rest consists of fat, blood vessels, nerves and protein. Humans have the largest brain to body size and a fully awake brain gives off enough energy to light a light bulb. God gave us all a brain. If your brain is fully functioning that means that you have much more than you think you have. You have the ability to think, plan, and execute ideas. But it's all a choice. You can choose to doubt yourself, you can choose to let obstacles and setbacks hold you back, you can choose to let situations and people's opinions of you stop you from moving forward to living up to your true wealth and potential.

Satan is the greatest deceiver that ever lives. He will tell you that you are worthless, that you are nobody and that nobody cares about you, nobody loves you. Those are all lies. You can do all things through Christ, you are more than a conqueror, you are a prized possession, you are from a royal priesthood, you are royalty, you are an heir or heiress, and you absolutely have money because you have an inheritance to draw from. You are rich, you are wealthy, you are beautiful, you are special, when God made you, He broke the mold, you are unique, you have gifts and talents, true wealth, just longing to come out. You are awesome, you are the head and not the tail, you have a mighty champion at your side, you have spiritual weapons to use to fight and win, you are victorious, a victor not a victim. I can go on and on.

The enemy wants you to be stuck in the same old places. He does not want you to leave poverty behind, he wants you to believe that you are poor and remain there so he can keep messing with you and stealing from you. He taps into your greatest power, your mind, and that's where he sets up shop, with strongholds, old beliefs, old habits, negative patterns of diet and thought, all to destroy, you, kill you early and steal your blessings. He did come to steal, destroy and kill after all, He has a job to do and he will continue to do it well if you do not put on the full armor of God. You will be a goner.

It's time for you to get dressed for battle. Get ready to tear down the strongholds that he has placed in your mind. Today is the day that the Lord has made and we are tearing down strongholds of fear and of failure. In Jesus name we tear them down right now. We will not be victims and captives of Satan anymore. We are already victorious. Who is it that overcomes this dark world? He that believes that Jesus is the son of God. It's time for you get out of my mind Satan, you cannot live here anymore. I am a child of the King and He came to give me a life! An abundant life at that. It's time for your diseases to leave my body in Jesus name. They cannot set up shop here anymore. I'm breaking free of disease today. I believe that and I will see this illness, blood disorder, cancer, diabetes, whatever disease it is, leave me starting from today. Amen. Jesus died on the cross for me, He shed his blood for me. He loves me. I can do ALL things through Christ who strengthens me.

Some of you reading this are battling mental disease, addictions, depression, pornography addiction, homosexuality, bad habits, divorce, promiscuity and more. Today God has sent me to tell you trust in the blood of Jesus. He did not just die for your sins, but for all your ailments. There is healing and victory in accepting the son of God. Say Jesus, come on into my mind, body and soul and clean me up Lord. I can't do this without you. I accept you as my deliverer, rescue me Lord. Amen.

It won't be easy, but you can break free from negative habits within thirty days. It takes a negative habit at least thirty days to form and you can break it in thirty days. Some might get the power right now to break it now. I pray that is you. Today is your day. Believe and it shall be so. The human brain has great power. Did you know that you can also change your blood in thirty days? Yes you can. There are plants that God created that clean your blood. Dandelion is king in that arena and burdock is like an emperor. God created a plant and herb for every ailment under the sun. ""Behold, I have given you every plant yielding seed that is on the face of all the earth, and every tree with seed in its fruit. You shall have them for food." (Genesis 1:29)

How then did people start getting all these diseases? Satan uses greed, love of money and love of instant gratification. So expensive drugs (which are derived from the same plants God made) were created, which most times have many side effects. Many of these expensive drugs do not cure, they alleviate the problem or the pain, without dealing with the root cause of the pain. Then there are lobbyists whose job is to lobby for government funds to research, develop and produce expensive pharmaceuticals.

True wealth also starts with gathering knowledge. That's why Solomon was considered the wisest and richest king. He asked God for wisdom. God gave him riches also. You can ask God for wisdom also, after all God is your father too. You do have an inheritance. Use your brain to let every cell in your body know that you have an inheritance and that you are rich. Pray for wisdom, knowledge and understanding. Seek righteousness and you will find, honor, prosperity and life. (Proverbs 21:21) True wealth comes when you seek righteousness.

For example, did you know that you can get sponsors to sponsor your dream? Whether you are a non profit or not there are big companies that will pay your expenses to go out and give speeches to help others, or put on events that help others. Knowledge is power to get things done. You take knowledge, creativity and develop your idea or dream, use wisdom to patent, trademark or copyright it, then you use courage to go out there and find a market for it. Determined and persistently, you sell what God gave you, your gift to the world, your talent manifested. If at first you don't succeed, you keep doing it over and over again, with focus, leaving distractions aside until you make it. Your true wealth is waiting. Time to get it out of your head, write it down, develop your plan, present the plan to God for **His blessing** and for ***provision for the vision***, then make sure you do your research and development, find a market and get your products, books and or services out there. The world needs your light.

4

Show Me the Money

Many who are suffering in poverty and lack can't see their wealth. They see with regular eyes that their bank account is overdrawn, that their wallets are empty, and maybe for some there is no meat in the fridge. They see no car in their driveway, or no gas in the car in the driveway, for some there is no driveway because there is no house or property.

As long as I have faith, I will always be a rich woman. People can take away money and gold from you but they cannot take away your faith. I prefer faith over money. With faith I can get anything I desire. My God spoke to my spirit a long time ago that I will be more charmed than Oprah. I constantly see how that's going to happen. I am getting closer to this prophecy each day because I know it's going to happen. Abraham waited all his life for God's promise to materialize. "According to your faith so be it unto you." (Matthew 9:29) Abraham did not see the ram in the bush when He was told to sacrifice his son Isaac. He was going on blind faith, following what God told him to do. Isaac when he had to uproot and relocate his entire family did not doubt God that he would find a place to live. He stepped out and kept it moving until he found something and it was so much room that he named it

Rehoboth, broad space. He didn't really know where he was going, but he kept on going, he didn't know if he would make it there, but he kept going. (Genesis 26:2) For those with no meat in the fridge, lentils are an excellent source of protein and is delicious in soup. You can feed a whole family with a big bag of lentils. Your family will be healthier and stronger too because plant protein is much better than meat protein. Vegetables and fruits are much healthier than expensive lobster, pies, cakes and red meat. No juice? Water is much better anyway. Your family will have fewer health problems, less cavities and they will be as strong as a bull.

No car as yet? Get a picture of the car you would like and put it on your fridge or a place where you can see it daily. Meditate and pray about being blessed with a car to help you and your family get around. In the meantime, go out and walk, enjoy the exercise, enjoy the fresh air, enjoy the sun nourishing you with vitamin D. I remember when I did not have a car. I was working at a newspaper selling advertising at the time. Well, I got the biggest check from not having a car because I chose to visit businesses close to public transportation, easy to get to and from. I went into a medical facility and made a sale for $12,000. Not having a car can work to your advantage. You can save money from not having a car. You save by not paying for gas, insurance, car wash, repairs and maintenance. You get better health by getting more exercise and more vitamin D.

For others who may have money, they see no one to love them, no one they can trust, no happiness, maybe no family. These are the folks who may have money but without love, peace of mind health and happiness the money is just worthless paper, a "social contrivance."

Since they cannot hug the money on a cold night, they sometimes dream of having someone to love them for them and not what they have in the bank. That's why I prefer faith over money. You see money cannot buy lots of things but faith can. Faith can get you a husband or a wife. I got my husband through faith. I manifested him up through my faith. I wrote down exactly the kind of man I would like to re-marry and I got exactly what I was asking for. Faith can get you happiness, love, wisdom, good health, wealth, understanding, all the things that money cannot buy.

If you cannot see money because its physical presence is not yet there to be seen, let's explore some real life examples on how to manifest money from nothing.

First you need pen and paper. Then you write the idea down. What do you want to do with your life? What is your burning passion? Pretend that Oprah came into your life and said she will back your ventures. What would you do with this blessing? What would you do if you had a rich backer, an angel investor? Someone that believed in you so much that he allows you to still breathe and he sent someone, a savior, to die for you, to lay down his life, so you can live an abundant life.

Believing that you have a rich investor or backer makes all the difference. Once I wanted to put on a gala to raise funds for our community center. The problem was that I had no funds to get started. But the solution was that I believed that God would send the money. My eyes of faith saw at least $20000. My bank account balance was negative $12.00. So I put a free ad out there for a volunteer on one of the many free volunteer websites. I requested a volunteer event planner. I got one with amazing qualifications. We met and we started to plan an amazing gala. She perceived that I had money because of the way I carry myself. I believe that I am an heiress and I have a very affluent father, who when I go to Him in prayer, He does not deny me. He does not give me a stone when I ask for bread. He loves me and above all things, He wants me to prosper and be in good health even as my soul prospers. Those are His exact words. See for yourself, read (3 John 1-2)

The event planner then scheduled meetings at three of the most extravagant banquet halls in town. We went to the first one, with its acres of well-manicured grounds, cobbled driveway, waterfalls and entered into a most delightful marble foyer. A white gloved, tuxedo clad attendant ushered us in graciously. The foyer area was quite large with very high chandelier lit ceilings and gigantic oil paintings.

I did not hesitate or look ill at ease. I smiled because of the beautiful surroundings and went to meet the man in charge of renting the space.

He asked why we were putting on the event. We told him about the community center in the 'hood' that provided tutoring for low income children and autistic teens as well as computer literacy classes for adults. He was impressed with our work and told us that he himself was an orphan that had to sleep in cars and fend for himself because he had no one to care for him.

He gave us as low a rate as he could and said we could send the deposit whenever we were able to. That worked out fine for us, because we had no deposit. We didn't choose the other halls, because they were far away from the community center and we felt that there was something magical about this banquet hall overlooking a state park. So we booked the day for the gala at a price of about $40 per plate per guests. We anticipated 200 guests paying $100 each for tickets.

After expenses such as awards, floral arrangements, invitations, giveaway bags and such we could still make a tidy profit for the community center.

We honored about 30 people in the community. One of them worked for a large bank. Because we started early about four months before the event date, we were able to ask for sponsors. The lady at the bank, became one of our sponsors and paid for 10 tickets as well. That was our deposit for the hall and money to order awards and organize the event. We went out to businesses, restaurants, airlines... and asked for in kind donations for the gala. We got gift certificates, airline tickets, spa certificates and more which we raffled off at the event and some we auctioned off at a private online auction. One person, a chef, auctioned off his services for a romantic weekend and that sold for $400. Another business, the exotic Dream Castle Villa, in Montego Bay,

Jamaica, West Indies sent a gift certificate which together with the airline vouchers we auctioned off for about $3200.

The day of the event came and we had an issue. Most of the money was to be collected at the door. There was an even bigger problem. There was a snow blizzard in the forecast for that day. I was very calm. I knew that God did not bring me all this way by faith for nothing. I believed that the people would come, so I did not cancel or reschedule. I went ahead and the people came and we actually made about $20,000 when all was said and done. You could do it too. When you step out on faith God always sends a parachute. Sometimes you get a lesson too. Failure often provides knowledge on better ways to do something. So don't be afraid that you fail.

When you do things that can enrich people's lives, that

is akin to pursuing righteousness. The bible says if you pursue doing right, prosperity, honor and life will follow. If you just do things for your selfish gains, you might not necessarily have the blessing or the favor. If you are selling drugs, you might make fast money, but you are killing people's minds, destroying families and you may end up dead or in jail. That's Satan's way. But if you try it God's way, the money might sometimes be slow, you might not see it, but it lasts forever. When you have God's blessing, you will always be successful, blessed coming and going. You may slip or fail sometimes, it won't always be smooth sailing, but those times or time when you fail, will teach you valuable lessons, plus Father is always there to pick you up, so don't ever stay down. Get back up and try again.

Sometimes when I fall or feel sad, I lift up my hands to the Heavenly King and He lifts me up in spirit. Do you remember when you were small and you wanted your dad or mom to pick you up and hold you in their arms? It works the same with God, you put your hands up and look unto the hills (heaven) and He will pick you up. Give your life to God, accept and believe that Jesus is the son of God and you will always be victorious, no matter what. (1 John 5:5)

5

The Plans of the Diligent Lead to Profit

Yesterday, I attended my CPA's customer appreciation luncheon. It was wonderful to network with all of their other business clients. There was a gentlemen from a major insurance company that spoke about the tremendous value of planning.

He illustrated by using the examples of partners in

business who had no formal agreement in writing. What if one partner fell sick? Would he or she be entitled to the profit sharing for the rest of his life even if he did not go back out to work in the business? If no formal plans were drawn up, that would be the case indeed. While the other partner sweated and grew the business, the other would be laying up and entitled to half since there were no formal contingency plans.

A major downfall of people of African descent is their lack of proper planning, especially in the area of life insurance. Like my buddy Bill, a partner at NY Life, always asks, "Does your cell phone have insurance and you don't?" Do we value our cell phone, or our cars more than our largest resource, our life?

Death is inevitable. Making sure you have ample insurance creates wealth for future generations. They inherit something to start a business, a franchise or buy real estate.

Small businesses especially do not plan well enough. For example, in family owned and operated businesses, the parents may have have no clear cut plans about who takes over the business when they die or if they fall ill.

The bible specifically says that "the plans of the diligent lead to profit, as surely as haste leads to poverty." Proverbs 21:5. The New Living Translation puts it this way: "Good planning and hard work lead to prosperity, but hasty shortcuts lead to poverty."

Many people are always looking for shortcuts to getting rich. We know that life is not always fair and that the rich continue to get richer while the poor get poorer. Can this be due to poor planning? For example, I have two friends who are in real estate. One is well off and the other is always scrambling to find her way financially.

My friend who is well off, has invested time and effort into real estate as his career. Everyone knows he is a broker. He has a steady book of business. He is seriously entrenched in real estate. He is focused on finding, listing and selling homes. My other friend is heavily into network marketing. She loves it and every six months or so, she joins a new network marketing company and proclaims how great their benefits are to everyone she can speak to. Because her focus is off, she is successful at neither. She makes a little money here and there from both. So she keeps struggling and wondering why she must struggle so. She has also adopted a new 'exotic' religion and does not claim herself as a Christian anymore. Meanwhile my other friend, remains grounded in his career and his Christian faith.

It's not that network marketing is bad. It is someone's

idea to create wealth for themselves and their families and they get many others to buy into this dream of creating wealth quickly. I suggested to my friend that there is a company that allows her to create residual income while growing her career in real estate. That company is Exit Realty. You get network marketing and you get a real estate career.

I have another friend, a bishop, who has a great company and worldwide ministry. If he focuses on growing his company, he would be well positioned to make millions. Instead he got sidetracked by a network marketing company, and has turned his energy over to making their company a roaring success rather than focus on his dream of becoming a roaring success. Now his great business has been sidetracked and is tottering.

The originality of your business, your passion and sweat combined with your talents will make enough room for you and God will set you in a large place. Do not dilute your vision, do not get distracted, make plans on how you will get there and you will get there if you stay the course. Branching off into network marketing, takes away your focus, your energy, your time and your money. That was time, energy, money and focus that could have gone into your business. Network marketing also lessens the credibility of the person who always has a new business idea to sell you. When you see them coming, you want to get away from them, because you know that they have yet another network marketing idea to sell you. People don't like to be sold to. People want to do business with people they trust, people that are solid and grounded in their respective fields. People who have been in a certain field for a long time and have remained focused on their goals, always realize their goals and achieve much. Others are drawn to such people because of their stability. They have earned credibility in their field and they attract wealth and many blessings. Most serious business people do not have time for network marketing because they are extremely busy creating their own empire, building their own wealth, living their own dreams rather than diverting their attention to someone else's idea and business.

The fastest way to a point is a straight line. Countless times, while driving to some destination, especially when running late, I have been tempted to deviate from a sure route to try an unknown or little known shortcut. Often, the shortcut does not work out for me. I become later and a little lost too.

It's important to stay the course and not distracted, tempted or sidetracked into taking a route that is unknown. Satan knows our personalities, our strengths and our weaknesses. He uses our weaknesses against us all the time. If he knows you are struggling, he will bring all sorts of get rich schemes in your face. These get rich schemes do require an investment and most times it is a substantial investment.

Most importantly, it requires time and energy. There are countless meetings and webinars that take your time way from your own business and dream. What is your plan for gaining true wealth? Do you want to invest in your business and have others invest in your business? Or do you want to put your business, your dreams on hold as you develop someone else's idea? Your idea or business is just as good as anyone's. All you need is focus, research, development, faith and a good plan. Stick with your dreams, don't abandon your own ship because someone else's ship looks better, sleeker and faster. If you keep putting time into developing your own ship, it will have no choice but to grow bigger, sleeker and shinier. Pretty soon, someone may want to buy your ship for millions of dollars.

Maybe your idea is to write a book. You need to plan to set aside time to do that. At least three hours or so a day. If you write three pages a day for thirty days you will have ninety double spaced pages. So you can write your manuscript in thirty days. If you want a thicker book because you have more to write about, you can continue writing for two more months, you will have two hundred and seventy pages. How much time are you investing to television or social media, although you have no product or service to promote? You can use that time wisely and turn hours into pages.

What about the time that you have to go convince everyone to try or join the newest network marketing business? If that's three hours per day, you can take a break from selling everyone else's dream for two months and write your book. Then you can go out there and sell your book with the same passion you sold the network marketing dream. You would make thousands, millions if your book becomes a best seller.

Books are cheap to write. All you need is pen and paper or for most writers, a laptop. But if you don't have a laptop, don't wait, start on pen and paper. Writing a book requires discipline. You cannot start today and go back to it two weeks later. You would have forgotten your train of thought by then. You have to keep it moving. Writing every day until the book is complete, stimulates your mind. You must be determined to make a life change for yourself and to change the lives of many others. When you write it is not for you. You hope you are not the only one who will read your book. You are writing to hopefully help millions of people worldwide who need guidance or inspiration in certain areas of their life, for which you happen to be an expert because you have been there and done that countless times.

Lastly, write a marketing plan for your book or for your business. Who will be your niche market? Exactly what demographic of people would want to read your book or to buy what you are selling. Where do those people live? In what kind of houses do they live? What are their hobbies? What is their income range? Are they married or single? Do they have children or have no children? Do they care about their health?

Get to know your target market intimately and you will be able to satisfy their minds, bodies and spirits.

I have seen people invest their life savings in businesses that they did no research and development for. They opened up hastily in areas where the residents were not known to buy those products or services. For example, opening a spa in a poor area where the people cannot afford luxuries such as dining out, would be a bad idea, because who would come? Also, can you provide parking? Location is everything is business. Do your market research well before you spend money to open a business. If you are buying raw land, spend money on getting an engineer's report. The land may look good to the naked eye but it may be 'unbuildable'. It may have been a dump or have contaminated soil. Likewise, if you are buying a home, an engineer's report is crucial so that you do not get stuck with property that has major plumbing or heating issues. Do your homework and take your time, even though you are so excited about opening a business or becoming a homeowner. Be diligent and take your time so you can be prosperous.

Remember an old West Indian adage, "Hurry birds don't build good nests," or take it straight from the book of Proverbs, written by the wisest king, "Haste leads to poverty."

6

Where There is a Will There is a Way

I know many people who wait for the right time to do everything. There is never a right time. Plan, research and do what you can today. For some tomorrow never comes. So many people die with their knowledge in their heads. I have heard so many excuses for people not living their dreams. The number one reason is of course, "I don't have the capital to start," followed by "I don't have the time." Some people tell me they are waiting to lose weight before they can begin living the abundant life that Jesus came into this world to give them. Some say they are waiting to fix their teeth, waiting until they fix their credit, waiting until they get married, waiting until, until, until………………………..

When we move forward with God on our side, He makes a way for us every time. Consider the Israelites when Moses got them out of Egypt. They didn't think that they would make it. But God made a way for them to escape. When Pharaoh came after them, God parted the Red Sea and made a path for them to go through. It's the same God we serve, a BIG GOD. Advance even if you don't see a way. You will be surprised at how often God will clear the way for you to go through. Many people don't believe they will be victorious and so they don't press on. They give up or do not start because they don't see the resources. But God will send people with resources, who have the ability to clear hurdles. When we put our trust and faith in God, it pleases Him and He sends back-up to help us move mountains.

We can do all things through Christ who strengthens us. (Phil. 4:13.) Our faith in God, when we take Jesus as our partner, as our angel investor, as our best friend, as our advisor, as our counsellor, as our covering, as the wind beneath our wings, can achieve many impossible feats. When I went to buy my first house, the bank turned me down. They said I did not make enough money, that my credit was not strong enough, that there was no way I could get the documents they required. Well, I proved them wrong, because the Lord had already told me that I would get a home and my friends at St. Matthew's church had already sent me a key through the mail, symbolic of keys to my first home.

I believed that I would get that new home. When the

bank said no, I informed them that God had already said yes. I refused to give up. I asked them for the list of documents that was required of me. Everything on that list seemed impossible, especially the commission guarantee. Since I was a salesperson at the time, I was paid commission on sales. They asked for a letter guaranteeing my commission at a certain amount each money. They said that was the only way I would qualify.

Well, it just so happened that the job had a commission guarantee at that specific time, since I had just started. They did guarantee me a commission but for *a limited time only*, which I instructed my manager not to mention in the letter that said my commission of a certain amount was guaranteed. They asked for other impossible documents which for some reason God allowed me to produce. The day of closing came and I did not have enough money to close. But I still went.

They eventually decided to take a postdated check from me, because I did not have the closing costs. I could have decided early on not to press on, but my pressing on resulted in me getting the keys to my four bedroom home.

God will make a way for us when we press on. Satan's job is to place many obstacles to discourage us from pressing on. He does not care who he uses or what he uses. He is intent on destroying our lives, by any means necessary, be it divorce, poverty, addictions, bad habits, sickness and disease, physical or mental.

In marriages, Satan will work to weaken one partner and to point out that person's weaknesses to the stronger spouse. Then he will send temptation in the form of someone strong to entice the spouse and to emphasize the weaknesses of the other. The grass will look greener on the other side and the spouse is then tempted to jump ship. When that happens, Satan is glorified. He is especially looking to destroy family units because he is anti -family. If he can divide and conquer he will be successful at tearing down each member of the family by messing with their mind and emotions. Satan often tries to use the man's weaknesses against him. He will cause the man to lose his livelihood so that financial woes enter the marriage. A high percentage of marriages fail because of financial problems. A higher percent because of infidelity. Because your spouse does not have money does not make him or her worthless, despite popular opinion. If that spouse has a plan and works that plan with laser like focus he or she can became solvent again. It's very difficult when it's the man who is the party without income or money, because women want a provider, their main need in a relationship is for security. Women like to be wined and dined, we like romance. We do not enjoy being the breadwinners and having to support our family, then having to be the nurturers as well. It impacts our lovemaking if we have to constantly give and nothing is being poured back into our lives, financially, spiritually or emotionally. That causes a drain on our emotions, which causes undue stress and can lead to illnesses.

Men have a need for physical contact, intimacy primarily. But if they are not able to provide security, their wife does not feel like giving sex and intimacy, because her needs are not being met. So we have two people in a marriage not getting what they desire the most. Then Satan often will showcase a man who is an excellent provider and the woman will be drawn to that man because he is king of his jungle and on top of his game. Then he goes for the jugular, if that wife sleeps with the successful man, the marriage begins to crumble and the wife feels more in tune with the new man.

Sometimes it's the other way around. Sometimes the husband goes out and finds a new love, a woman who will give him the intimacy he craves. Often it's the woman who is weak, has no job, has no money and no influence. (Those times are changing fast.) The husband becomes extremely bored with her and may be tempted to go outside the marriage to find a more dynamic woman. Leaving a broken marriage in the wake. Hold on in every instance, help is on the way. God will make a way. Do not get weary of doing good, in due season you will reap if you do not faint. He will give you wings to soar. Things will get better. Use eyes of faith to see beyond not just see the current circumstance but that with prayer, your situation will change. Amen

7

Bootstrapper Extraordinaire

Businessdictionary.com defines bootstrapping: 1. Building a business out of very little or virtually nothing. Boot strappers rely usually on personal income and savings, sweat equity, lowest possible operating costs, fast inventory turnaround, and a cash-only approach to selling. Many of today's largest corporations (such as Apple computer, Clorox Co., Coca Cola, Dell Computer, Hewlett-Packard, Microsoft) began as boot-strapped ventures. Most of world's startups still follow this road; either because there is no alternative, or because of the unmatched control and independence it offers.

There are millions of millionaires who brought themselves up by the bootstraps. Their parents had no money, they had no money and they started businesses with no money. They used grit and faith and believed in themselves. They kept going when others folded, they invented things, they figured out ways to do things better and faster than others and they profited. They focused excessively on the question: How can I add value to my customer? It's the same question, what can I bring to the market that people will need or have an innate desire to purchase? How can I entertain in a different way that millions will come to watch me perform?

So you have no capital, no money to start a business. I know people who invested their welfare checks, their unemployment checks or their social security checks to start their business. I am one of those people. First you will need discipline, since you don't have much money. Secondly, you will need focus to zoom in on what people need or want more of and a profitable way for you to supply that demand.

Next, build a business that will last, tweak it constantly so your baby does not become irrelevant. Don't just start a business to get rich by selling it for big bucks. Build a business that could really supply a need and that has longevity.

Don't be afraid to be the head chef, the dishwasher and the cleaner. Embrace the fact that at first you won't have money to hire staff. Read more books, research and invest in technology to make your jobs easier. Put systems in place so you can cover each demand that may arise. Learn to multi-task. Try to get a business partner so you have someone to help and bounce ideas off. When you do hire staff, train them well, identify their strengths and weaknesses early on so they can be most effective.

Manage your bills and cash flow well by adopting an accounting system. Hire a CPA or accountant or take an accounting class so you can be on top of your cash flow.

You can do much more than you think you can with the little that you have. It requires a plan, prayer, faith, discipline and determination to succeed. Avoid those get rich schemes and prepare to work hard and smart at making your business a success. Don't deviate from your path. Many people will come and try to get you to jump ship, especially if you have a dynamic personality and are a great people person. Your ability to articulate well and your gregarious nature should not succumb to excessive spending and willy- nilly investments lest your indiscipline lead to weakness and failure. People will come to you telling you to come over to their business, which promises to be the next big thing. They will tell you it is a no brainer, that you are bound to succeed. When you ask them the plan, or tell them that you are busy building your own business or your dream, they will tell you that you are perfect for the business they are building and that you are a great match. Don't be an easy target. Don't fall for the distraction of time and money. This is simply someone coming to derail you from you becoming the next big thing. They are essentially saying to you that the idea or business that they are selling is better than yours. If they got you to sign up and start working for them, then you know what they say, suckers are born by the minute. It requires discipline to stay on track. When those people come trying to derail you, start selling them your business or dream and let them buy something from you or convince them to go out there and sell your products and services. Tell them they are a natural at it. You can convince them to be your public relations and sales representative by showing them the way to make money and tall profits.

Every multi-level marketing business is based on 'IF'. If you get five people to join in on this you will qualify to go to the next level and make X amount of dollars. If you get thousands of people to buy into your business at $400 each, plus pay you $50 each month, yes, you will be a billionaire in a very short space of time. I would like to start my own multi-level marketing business with a useful product for women.

8

Restoring the Broken

Millions of people worldwide often use the phrase, "I'm broke." Today God will show you how to repair and restore broken lives or even broken finances. The book of Nehemiah is not just about repairing the broken walls and gates of the mystical city, Jerusalem. This book contains guidance on restoring and fixing mankind's brokenness.

In the book of Nehemiah 1: 3-7, Nehemiah inquires and learns about the state of the exiles and Jerusalem's walls. "They said to me, "Things are not going well for those who returned to the province of Judah. They are in great trouble and disgrace. The wall of Jerusalem has been torn down, and the gates have been destroyed by fire……When I heard this, I sat down and wept. In fact, for days I mourned, fasted, and prayed to the God of heaven. Then I said, "O LORD, God of heaven, the great and awesome God who keeps his covenant of unfailing love with those who love him and obey his commands, listen to my prayer! Look down and see me praying night and day for your people Israel. I confess that we have sinned against you. Yes, even my own family and I have sinned! We have sinned terribly by not obeying the commands, decrees, and regulations that you gave us through your servant Moses."

Observe how Nehemiah prayed. He first saluted the greatness of God and then he took some responsibility for the sin of his people. That is the first step to restoring brokenness. Take responsibility for your shortcomings or for your sins without blaming others. Second step, pour out your heart to God. Cry if you want too, Nehemiah fasted, wept, prayed and for days he mourned.

Many situations can leave us financially broke, mentally, physically and spiritually broken and in despair. For some it's a divorce, for others rape, others grapple with addictions, homosexuality, bisexuality, promiscuity, pornography, being overly critical of others but rest assured, whatever it is that broke you down, we cannot fix on our own, we need God's help.

Nehemiah prayed for God's help. He prayed for favor with King Artaxerxes in whose court he was employed as a cup bearer. That was a dangerous job and a very trustworthy job. Although Nehemiah had found out about the broken walls and destroyed gates of Jerusalem in the late fall, it was not until spring time that he got an opportunity to speak to the king about the problem that bothered him. He prayed and he waited for God. The issue weighed on him so heavily that it showed on his face and the king asked him what was wrong.

The king listened and asked Nehemiah what he wanted. Nehemiah knew exactly what he needed, after all he had been meditating and praying about the situation day and night. What's interesting is that Nehemiah was a stand-up guy. He could have stayed in the safe employ of the king, instead of risking his life to go and rebuild the walls and gates of Jerusalem. Instead, he took action and stepped up to the plate without anyone telling him to or asking him to.

Third step to repairing your brokenness: Step out on a

limb. Be courageous and take action. Don't just keep despairing about the problem, go to someone that can help. Make every effort to repair your brokenness. Don't let depression and hopelessness paralyze you from taking action. With God's help all things become possible. Your best efforts plus God's favor will make you fruitful and productive again.

Nehemiah had a plan. He asked the king for timber from the king's forest. He also asked for a royal envoy to see him safely there and letters from the king to give to the officials in Jerusalem ensuring diplomatic immunity and full cooperation. He got all he asked for, although it was a lot. Nehemiah was gone for twelve years, so he also got paid time off. Think big, ask big, we serve a big God.

When Nehemiah got to Jerusalem, he rested for about three days and then went by himself to see the actual condition and formulate a plan for the rebuilding. He then gathered the priests of Jerusalem, the exiles and inspired them to help in restoring the broken city. This is the fourth key to restoring broken lives, get some type of team together. Get the support of family and or community. Nehemiah got everyone to come out and rebuild the gates to the city of God.

Fifth, expect opposition and have a winning strategy so they don't stop you. There were haters back in Nehemiah's time. Their job is to distract people from fulfilling their purpose, from rebuilding their lives. Don't stop working, keep up your best efforts, regardless of their taunts or threats. Don't be afraid of them. Nehemiah didn't listen to them and he put half of the builders to guard the city to stop the haters from burning it down. At certain points people were building with one hand and had a weapon in the other.

The gates of Jerusalem have long been symbolic of

restoration and healing. Jerusalem is where Jesus was born. It is prophesied that it is where the Messiah will return to judge the living and the dead. These gates have much to teach us. The gates are prophetically and symbolically named. They have spiritual meaning to help the lost reclaim victory through Jesus Christ. Studying the spiritual meaning of these gates open the way for full restoration for anyone feeling broken, depressed, burnt out and destroyed.

The first gate that Nehemiah tells us about is the Sheep Gate. (Nehemiah 3:1) Sheep is symbolic of sacrifice, sheep also need shepherds to guide them. Jesus is the ultimate shepherd, He is our guide to restoring broken lives. Through Christ we can end old habits that lead to poverty and misery and we can make plans to living productive, abundant lives.

The second gate was the Fish Gate which symbolizes

witnessing to others. Jesus said we will be fishers of men. We are our brothers' keepers. We must not just wait for preachers and leaders to guide people, we each can counsel, evangelize, guide others to salvation. We can be leaders regardless of our station in life. We each have a special gift to share with the world. Let that light shine and God will make a way for you. The more you give of yourself, of your gift, the more prosperous you shall be and the more room God will make for you.

The third gate was the Old City Gate, symbolizing old ways of truth. Embracing old wisdom versus new fast ways. Let us strive to be honest because integrity and character will last forever. When you have integrity and character, people trust you and will do business with you faster than they would do business with someone who is known for making bad decisions or with someone who lies and cheats. Let your word be your bond and you will make more money because of a good reputation. People will also give you goods on credit because they know you are a reputable person.

The fourth gate was the Valley Gate symbolizing humility. God resists the proud and helps the humble. Don't always want to be right. We all make mistakes, be humble and apologize when you do. Pride goes before a fall. So if you want to fall, take pride with you.

The fifth gate was the Dung Gate symbolizing elimination of refuse. Some people refuse to give up the filth in their lives. If you hold on to filth you will stink. You have to let it go. Letting go of bad habits is very hard, because old habits die hard. But be encouraged, you can start a new habit by doing something good each day for 30 days. If you want to break a bad habit, don't continue to hang out with people who encourage you to continue on with the habit or who still have the same bad habit. Find other more wholesome friends and family. If you are trying to stop drinking or smoking, don't hang around drinkers and smokers. Put some effort and sweat into repairing your brokenness. You have work to do. Nothing good will come easy, you have a part to play.

The sixth gate was the Fountain Gate which symbolizes a Holy Spirit filled life that overflows to help guide others. It comes after the Dung Gate, so get the poo out of your life and welcome in the Holy Spirit which washes us clean. When we are spirit filled, we get revelation from God himself. He shows us many wonderful things and gives us discernment to read into the hearts of men.

The seventh gate was the Water Gate, which symbolizes the word of God. Studying the word of God allows us to break chains and sets us free to live an abundant life.

The bible says that faith comes by hearing the word of God. Hearing the word, studying the word, builds knowledge of God and faith. We learn principles and get strategies to empower us.

The eight gate was the horse gate symbolizing battle and spiritual warfare, which we must be dressed and ready for at all times. Ephesians 6 says to put on the full armor of God, taking the shield of faith with which we can extinguish all the fiery darts of the enemy.

The ninth gate, the East Gate, is perhaps one of the most symbolic and meaningful gate. It is still there today and faces the rising sun. It represents hope and it sometimes called the Gate of Eternal Life. It is believed this is the gate that Jesus used to enter Jerusalem when he came riding on a donkey. This is the gate that the Messiah will return through. It is sometimes called the gate of Mercy. Have hope, don't give up, the longer you hang on the better it will be for you. It is so easy to give up and let go, it takes strength, both mentally and physically, to hold on.

The tenth gate was called the Inspection Gate, reminding us that we must give account of our lives. This gate reminds us that there will be a judgement day. After that, Nehemiah's account takes us back to the Sheep Gate and ends there. This symbolizes our return to the Lord. A return to the fold, led by the great shepherd, Jesus, the Lion of Judah, the Lamb of God whose life was sacrificed for us.

It's time to repair your gates, with God's help there is hope that you will be restored, just have the discipline and courage to follow through and perseverance to continue until all your walls are repaired. Nehemiah and the exiles were motivated and they repaired those walls while being under attack, in fifty two days. You can do the same. Put in the effort and go for it. God will make a way for you.

9

The Power of Faith

The book of Nehemiah is the book of restoration.

There is a book in the bible that helps us to increase our faith. Hebrews is that book. "Faith is the substance of things hoped for the evidence of things not seen." (Hebrews 11:1) Abraham had the most faith in the world that we know of. He waited for over 80 years for God's promise in his life to materialize. The world that we are living in today, with its instant gratification and microwave mentality, could never live up to that. I consider myself to have big faith but I honestly don't know if I can wait eighty years. At the end of two years of marriage many wonder if they married the right person. Many others file for divorce because they don't see results that the marriage is working.

Still others give up on their dreams because financially they are weak. For faith to move mountains, it must be unshakeable. Faith is not just a noun it is also a verb to me because unless you tie action, effort and determination to faith it does not work.

Many people simply hold on without taking consistent steps to rectify a bad situation. They often get paralyzed by fear of the unknown and stay stuck. When a vehicle gets stuck, think about the immense effort needed to get that vehicle out of the hole. We have to get several people to push the vehicle out of the rut. We call for back up, a tow truck, the police, because the vehicle is disabled and we need help to get it out of the rut. So too, when a human being gets in a rut, it's hard to get out unless similar great efforts are employed. We must call for back up, we must roll up our sleeves and push like we never pushed before until we get out. It is imperative that we get out of the rut because our life is more important than any stuck vehicle. Just like people depend on a vehicle to get around, people are depending on us to provide for ourselves and family. The same way we don't leave our vehicle in the rut is the same way we should not remain in any rut. Find a way to get out of the rut. If we stay in the rut, be it a financial rut, unemployment rut, health rut, sin rut, addiction rut, bitterness of spirit rut, envy and jealousy rut, malicious and backbiting rut, whatever type of rut it is, if you stay there you will get rusty and slowly die. Your mind will slow down, you will feel resigned and unhappy, and you will feel slightly bitter when you see people enjoying life. You will not be motivated to enjoy life because you are stuck in the rut. You will invite others into the rut, into your misery and they will begin to hate you eventually because no one wants to live in a rut. A rut is supposed to be a very temporary place that many have made into a permanent lifestyle. It became habitual to stay down because when you fell into the rut, you cried but no one heard, you gave up eventually and resigned yourself to staying there.

Well today is the day that God had decreed and declared that you are to leap out of that rut with the supernatural power of the son of God. Jesus has heard your cries and the angel of mercy is going to pull you out of that rut beginning today. That rut no longer defines you, you have outgrown it. You deserve to enjoy life not wallow in misery and not let anyone hold you down any longer.

Get a pen and paper and write down who you can call to help you out of the rut. These should be anointed spiritual people who will speak faith and action into your mind, body and spirit. Know who to call. Call on people who are out there moving on a mighty mission to save souls. After you give them a synopsis of how you got in the rut, why you never could seem to get out of the rut, then listen to what they have to say to you. Their words may burn you if they speak truth. Hear them to the end, write down what they say. Ask them for recommended steps to get out of the rut that you are in and then follow those steps religiously.

In the book of Nehemiah, the spiritual meaning of the gates of the sacred city Jerusalem showed us tangible steps to take to restore broken down lives. The first step was to confess the sin that got you in the rut without blaming anyone. Technically, Nehemiah was not responsible for the sins that left Jerusalem a burnt out destroyed city, but still he confessed the sins of his people, his family and said he was sorry for that.

To use faith as an action plan to get you out of any rut or to get you to the financial freedom you desire, you have to put some effort into it. If you don't like work, thinking, planning nor following up diligently, then financial freedom may come only by gambling. So if that was your strategy to achieve financial freedom, knock yourself out but expect to stay in a rut. Winning the lottery is a fool's financial strategy. Yes it may happen, but the chances are extremely slim. You could be putting your energy into thinking, planning and working a strategic plan.

Business people take calculated risks. People who work a nine to five are not the biggest risk takers. They want a steady pay check and that's alright. But you can still think of ways to invest that paycheck so that you won't be working for the man till you die. There is an invention in each and every one of us. Put some thought, some effort and persistence into thinking of an app or a product or service that can really help people. Maybe it's a book or a song that can really transform people's lives. Your idea can change the world, if you have enough faith to act on it and carry it through.

Sometimes the rut becomes so comfortable though. Some grow accustomed to living from paycheck to paycheck. Some try something else and get burned and go right back in their hole. The effort was there, the persistence was lacking. Some people are afraid to stick their head out of the hole, lest it gets chopped off, these lack courage, so they stay in the miserable hole. Some people fail to prepare a strategic plan to get out of the hole and they come out only to fall right back in. Then there are those who make a plan but do not add any consistency of effort, so their plan falls to pieces because of lack of execution and follow through.

Here are some steps to get out of any financial woe or rut and to soar like an eagle:

- Pray for supernatural help and favor
- Confess your shortcomings, your sins, your faults, bad habits that get in the way of your success
- Apologize for these shortcomings without blaming anyone, take full responsibility
- Write or draw a plan of strategic action that you know can pull you out of the rut and lead to success. What are your areas of expertise?

What are you passionate about? Who do you know?

- Research and write down some names of people and or organizations who can push you, pull you out of the rut and propel you to success. You will find names of such people at Small Business Administration website, chambers of commerce, economic development centers, government offices, churches with ministers who care, Linked in, Facebook even Instagram. Reach out to them, try to make an appointment and discuss your strategic plan of action that can benefit them and you.
- After the meeting, follow up. Most times in sales, you don't get a sale on the first visit,

maybe the second or the third sometimes on the seventh visit.

- Use integrity and character at all times. If people can trust you, they will give you money or buy whatever you're selling. People do business with people they like and trust.
- Believe in yourself. You can do whatever you put your mind to do. Don't stop until you get what you want.

Without faith it is impossible to please God. We must absolutely jump in order for our Godly parachute to open. That leap of faith should be planned wisely and executed with as much precision as we can muster. Know that you have a mighty champion at your side and keep pressing on towards the prize.

10

Faith versus Money

Would you rather have big faith or big money?

Faith as a substance is a little known resource. It is an underestimated resource because many do not know of faith's power and value. I would prefer to have big faith than big money because money can finish, but faith is infinite. When you have big faith you can get the millions. Faith has the ability to level the playing field between people born with a gold spoon in their mouths and the poor.

Faith + Talent + Courage + Plan + Effort + Persistence = Success

Nowhere in this equation is money mentioned. You can make yourself a success without money. It takes faith. Distraction from your goals slow you down. The fastest way to a point is a straight line. God has already given you all the tools you need to prosper. A functioning brain to think and to gather wisdom; ears to hear the Word and take in knowledge; eyes to see and read the Word; feet to get moving; hands to make and create things, to eat and to work; a mouth to speak intelligibly and eat healthy food to nourish your body so that you would stay strong. Reproductive organs to be fruitful and multiply. Every organ, every body part has a function that empowers us. That's why the bible says to remember the Lord thy God for it is He that giveth thee power to get wealth. (Deuteronomy 8:18) People don't know they have that much wealth and power, many are unaware of their true worth. The insurance companies will ask us, what is our net worth. My answer is at least $10 billion, which I don't say because then they want me to prove it. But my brain has high value because of all the inventions and ideas that are stored there that I am trying to get out into the world. I would say that our brain is worth about $1 billion. Then our eyes, our ears, our reproductive organs, kidneys, heart, legs, hands are all so valuable, I think that each individual is worth about $10 billion. We sell ourselves so short though. Most of us have no clue how much we are worth. We look at celebrities as having more worth than us. Celebrities have more money than us, yet many live miserable lives. If God came down and said, Simone, what do you want? How do you want me to bless you? I would answer more wisdom and faith that could move mountains. Do you see how those two can make you wealthier than King Solomon?

Why chase money when you can chase God? Chase righteousness and all things you desire will follow. The way this works is that as you chase after becoming a better person in God's sight, following His commandments, being obedient to His will, favor, goodness and mercy will chase you down until you have all that you desire.

Satan does not want you to recognize this power that you have because then he won't stand a chance. So what does he do? He distracts you, he tempts you mercilessly, until you fall and start feeling unworthy. Then your self-esteem drops because you feel unworthy. Once self-esteem levels dip low, so too does confidence in one's abilities and talents. You can't shake your money maker if you feel broken and in a rut. Sin was created to keep us down. But then God's plan for salvation really upset the enemy because Jesus redeemed and rescued us from sin by sacrificing his life for ours so that we can live an abundant life.

We can ask God to increase our faith and trust to know that things will work out for us in every situation. More money does not mean that things will work out, it might just do the opposite with more money. How about more faith to have a baby for those struggling with fertility issues? It pleases God immensely when we use our faith, not when we spend our money. When you please God you get favor to get all the desires of your heart. The love of money is the root of all evil. The love of faith is trusting God, which leads to happiness, joy and strength, all of which money cannot buy.

Have faith to meditate and ask God to show you some ideas or inventions that will solve a need for mankind and make you a billionaire. Then you can prove to the insurance company or anyone that asks you your net worth, that you really are a billionaire and not just in your head.

The more effort you put into your actions the more mountains you will be able to move by faith. I once published an independent community magazine where I wore many hats. I started with no money and sold ads to raise cash to cover the costs of publishing the magazine. It was hard work, because

I also wrote most of the articles as well. I did everything except the graphic design.

Well, I made good profits with the magazine but could have done better with a team. The best thing that happened because of me starting that magazine, was the people I met along the way. The magazine opened doors for me that would have never opened before when I had a regular job. I was picked up by the White House press and they sent me all the invites to cover President Barack Obama, First Lady Michelle Obama and the Obama administration. I was getting the Obama handshake without paying tens of thousands of dollars to do so. It was very encouraging to me as a small business owner to often be in the same room as the President of the United States of America.

I often took people with me to get the Obama

handshake and they were inspired as well. I learnt that great leaders inspire greatness in others. I met Pulitzer Prize winners, great African-American speakers and orators, such as, Toni Morrison, Cornell West, Amiri Baraka, Susan Taylor, Jon Bon Jovi and many, many more. The magazine was like a muse around town. My goings and comings inspired all who read it that they could start businesses that could open incredible doors for them, that they could write books, that they could put on events, seminars and workshops, even if they did not have money. I went to the schools and inspired the school children too, I showed them how to start a business, write and get published. I had started out in my hometown and now God has promoted me and is sending me to the entire world to inspire greatness in others. So I say to you,

"Namaste." (The divinity in me salutes the divinity in you.)

Things work when you put extra effort into it by preparing a business plan and marketing strategy. No matter where you are in the world, it's the same. Lack of planning will cause you to fail. If you have planned very well and still fail, consider it a lesson and learnt from it so next time you can do better. We put on a community event at a park on the last weekend of summer. It did not do very well because that was a weekend that everyone was trying to go somewhere. Also, though we had strong paid advertising; word of mouth and community engagement were not strong enough. So we learnt that next time, all these factors had to be addressed.

When you are organized things flow smoothly in all

areas of your life. Keep your files organized. Cleanliness is good for the soul, clutter makes one confused. If you cannot pay staff get interns. Working from home? There are virtual interns. Volunteers can also make your events spectacular. Strong faith is nothing but strong belief + strong effort.

I admire President Donald Trump. He had a strong marketing strategy that enabled him to win. Trump saw what worked with Obama's campaign, he saw Obama inspiring hope in millions of people who had lost hope. People from the wrong side of town, who had never voted, all came out of the woodwork and voted for Obama. Trump used the same strategy, on a different market of people. He went to the rural people, farmers, and people living in cute and not so cute trailers, working people who America had forgotten. People who were not minorities, were not getting any breaks, instead their jobs were outsourced to China and India. These people voted for Trump because he made them feel good about themselves. He gave them hope.

Without hope, we cannot win. Without faith, courage and effort we would not even try. Without persistence we won't keep going. Don't grow weary of doing good, because if you faint not, you will reap a harvest. (Galatians 6:9) Mrs. Hillary Clinton said that in her speech to her supporters after it was declared that Trump had won. We must keep up the fight. Victory and/or change is right around the corner. People do change, situations change. It may take a while but little tiny drops of water can fill a huge barrel.

I invented the "by faith credit card. " That's where I

did things for years, put on events, published books and magazines, with no money. I used the power of faith. Faith is like credit, the backer is God Almighty. He backs every by faith transaction. He credits your account with blessings and favor. People activate credit cards all the time, they even activate a welfare card but not many know that there is a by faith card just begging to be activated.

There is no limit on this card, do as much as you could with it, only make sure that all you do is for the good of the kingdom of God. Make sure that it is not for selfish gain and the by faith card will be honored everywhere you go. Unless you shop in hell. Satan definitely does not want any child of God to know about this by faith card, much less use it. He is a liar and a deceiver, so he wants you to believe that you are penniless and broke. He wants you to die with your wealth still in your mind. Don't be fooled by the enemy.

You can rise up from every negative situation. The enemy thought that they had killed and utterly destroyed Jesus. His resurrection surprised them all and now the enemy spends his time trying to discredit Jesus. Trying to make Jesus irrelevant. Trying to seduce people with exotic religions. Don't fall for that, Jesus is the answer and the bible the panacea for recovery and victory. It was through faith that Isaac moved into a new land and started over again, you can do the same. It was with faith that Joseph though imprisoned and treated wrongly for so many years, rose to the top. It was with faith that Naaman dipped in the water seven times and was healed of leprosy. It was through faith that Elijah went to the ravine and depended on the raven to feed him. We need faith to live for it is written that man shall not live by bread alone but by every word that comes forth from the word of God.

We are more than conquerors. Don't consider failure, keep going until you make it. God is on your side. Your talent will make room for you in this world. Don't be afraid to let your light shine. You have greatness within. It is time to let it come out. You are neither penniless nor poor. You are a child of the King, you have an inheritance. Don't let Satan fool you into believing that you are nobody. You are special, there is no one like you. Don't let Satan or anyone of his workers steal your inheritance. Don't sell yourself short because of the past, you are worth billions. You are a priceless model and what Satan meant for harm to kill you, destroy you, God will use to strengthen you and give you a testimony. Wear those scars proudly, you are a great warrior and it's not over yet because God has plans to prosper you. Stay on the course. Hold on tight, it may get bumpy and there may be some hurdles to jump over.

11

Ways to Make Money

Wherever you live there are ways that you can earn a living that will surpass your dreams, if you are willing to step out on faith, be courageous and put in time, effort and persistence. Here are some ideas, even if you have little or no money to invest.

1. Become a realtor. Save enough of your earnings to buy some real estate. Rent the rooms or offices. If you are a people's person, articulate and hardworking, this career will allow you to build and save huge amounts of income.
2. Write a short eBook over the weekend. Give it a catchy title, teach people how to do something that you're good at. Upload it to Amazon, give away a few copies and watch your sales build up. Write a series and see more income.
3. Invent a toy, game or kitchen gadget, or even an app. Think about something that will be useful and new. One lady invented see through bra straps. That could have been you... I invented the iCan, a soy massage candle that comes in five divine scents: iCan Heal, iCan Love Me, iCan Aspire, iCan Let Go and Let God and

the iCan- By Faith. It's a three in one candle, massage, aromatherapy and prayer candle.

4. Are you interested in motivational speaking? Are you good at inspiring or helping others? You can make DVD's or CD's of your speeches and sell them online and offline.

5. You can open any business supplying a good or service, maybe even a landscaping business, get minority certified and get a government or transit contract.

6. You can import a special or exotic product or spice, get a distributor for it and sell it in all the states of America.

7. How about a special juice or tea that you can bottle or box? It should have some special healing properties.

8. Are you an author? Would you like to be an author? You can get sponsors to sponsor your new book and speaking tour, as long as you will give out samples and promote the sponsor wherever you go. Prepare a game plan and a sponsorship package and go 'knock' on some sponsor doors.

9. You can start a multi-level marketing corporation. Know a product that is in high demand? People are buying it anyway, they need it or want it badly. Create a network for it and allow people to make money selling it. Hint: Think of things that people buy a lot of. Create a niche market.

10. Start a community newspaper or magazine and sell ads to businesses that need the exposure.

It's very cheap to print a newspaper. Magazines are much more expensive.

11. Are you a singer or in great physical shape? Sell CD's with your songs or DVD's with your exercise regimen.

12. Like to cook? Get a food handler's license and become a caterer. Develop a marketing strategy and cater to sales organizations, businesses and non-profits.

13. Into agriculture or do you like animals? Get two goats, male and female and breed them. Sell the kids. You can do this with pedigree dogs. Rottweilers are always in demand and each pup sells for about $400 - $500 dollars.

14. Turn your house into a bed and breakfast inn. If you live in a rural or suburban type area with lots of acreage, build a yurt and rent it out for

visitors. People like to stay in hotels that are unusual. Build a spacious, sound tree house and rent that out too. (Must have bathroom.) Put your apartment on Airbnb or homeaway.com and make some money.

15. Have a lot of land? Farm it by planting an easy vegetable or crop or by raising chickens. Organic chickens are very easy to rear. Sell the eggs. Organic eggs fetch a great price. Raise turkey, wild geese. Restaurants will buy from you. Get workers from the country or West Indies who know how to pluck the feathers off chickens fast.

16. Are you a pastor or minister? Get registered to be a marriage officiant, hang out at city hall where couples get their marriage licenses and give them your card. This may very well help

your ministry to grow as well. You don't need a license to sell your books on the streets. Check your state's requirements.

17. Are you an actor or actress? Put on a play, sell tickets, sell the DVD's to the play. Do this often and you will have many plays under your belt. Tyler Perry will have to move over.

18. Do you like being on television? Start a web series talk show interviewing interesting people. Get a following and get sponsors.

19. Like to videotape? Get some professional editing software and go around to all the business doing their short video commercial. This used to work, but now with Instagram, everyone is using a cell phone and taking video. However, there will always be people who want a properly filmed video.

20. Start some type of school or professional academy.

21. Start a professional membership organization, helping a particular group of people, develop a marketing plan to gain new members and shoot for the sky.

22. Make a unique sauce or food seasoning. Bottle it, get labels, barcodes and make sure you have the appropriate food handlers' approval from you city or state.

23. Are you popular or funny? Become a social media business wiz. Take pictures and post them, get a huge following then get sponsors who would pay you to post their clothing, products and services on your page.

24. Do you have cute or smart children or pets? Market them to be models, actors and/or

spokespersons of interested companies and for the movies. A friend of mine trained his cat to use the toilet and he took pictures and made a popular video.

25. Always make sure you have life insurance. Share some of these business ideas with your children. Even if you don't become a millionaire in your lifetime, you can pave the way for them by having life insurance. When you go home to be with the Lord, your children can have a start in life to start a business or even buy a franchise. African-Americans have the highest spending power in America but yet they are the least insured race in America. This means that no wealth is being transferred. The church often has to pay for the burial costs and the adult

children inherit debt rather than millions to buy real estate and start a business.

Saving money is very important. You can save by putting aside at least 10% of your paycheck each time you get paid. If you can save more, go for it. If you save $1000 each month for 12 months, you should be able to open a business by the next year. Set goals for yourself and stick to them. Scale down on your expenses. Do your own laundry for a year, forgo dry cleaning for a year, do your own hair for a year, do your own nails for a year, eat in for a year, no vacation for a year (try a staycation instead, maybe a short stay in a state you can easily drive too.) Cut your cable and watch movies online. Just lay low and focus for a year and save.

No job, no paycheck to save anything? Listen, you can always find something to do. It may seem beneath you to work at McDonald's or Walmart but honest work should not be beneath you. You can use honest work like this to hoist yourself up. Do not let despair paralyze you from moving quickly before serious depression sets in. Remember that a rolling stone gathers no moss. Keep moving, resist the temptation to stay in the house and be on the computer, unless income is coming in from you being on the computer. Get out there and do something. Gather some capital while you work at a diner or restaurant (think tips) and start up a business. If you are a stay at home husband with no income, then you are a burden on your wife and you probably won't have a wife for much longer. Women desire stability, security is their number one need. So if she does not feel secure around you, you are contributing to an unhappy marriage, stress and disease. Women do not thrive well in those situations. They won't be feeling sexy, they won't be feeling to make love, which is the man's first need in a marriage, intimacy. So there we have a stalemate (no pun intended.)

Likewise, if you are a stay at home wife, who won't go out and help your husband to build up and store wealth, then he may feel justified in looking for that type of woman outside the marriage.

I have come to understand that divorce does not happen overnight. Years of compromise, suffering and misery sometimes make a divorce a reality. Often one spouse is not paying keen attention to the signs of unhappiness and mostly they are not doing anything about it. Ministers, members of the clergy often have marital problems because they often have few avenues to turn to for help.

Also often, they get taken advantage of because the other spouse believes that the clergy spouse is God and have no human frailties or human desires. Ministers are men and women, we are often tempted, we have desires, we have weaknesses, as for me I have a strong belief in God, but many others are led away because they could not hold on. Although the bible says that we should consider trials pure joy and that we should enjoy longsuffering, there is no need for any spouse to test that verse by not addressing the needs of the other spouse. If you have two people in a marriage whose needs are not being met, they are candidates for Satan to pick on for destruction, clergy or not. Clergy get attacked more than the layman because if Satan could destroy the spiritual leader or put blemish on him or her, then their followers are left disappointed and disillusioned. This causes a decrease in church membership, because they will say, "Who can trust pastors anymore?"

We have a responsibility in marriage to look after the other's happiness. We should put effort into seeing and doing what makes our spouse happy. I read recently that if the purpose of marriage was happiness then everyone would be married. The real purpose of marriage is holiness. We want to live holy lives and set an example for our children and their children.

My point is that there are many situations that may contribute to you not being to save. You still have to do it if you want to reach your goals.

To be a millionaire takes faith and courage, ideas and products, discipline, sacrifice, some serious planning and persistence. Notice how I did not say money. Man makes the money. Which came first the chicken or the egg? The idea comes first it then manifests into money. We create the money, we create the harvests by planting seeds (literally) that grow with time into millions. (of trees that are cut down to make money.)

12

The Harvest

America is a place of great harvest, prosperity… Many nations come here to get a piece of the American pie. However, many Americans are depressed, oppressed, frustrated and living in lack. They have lost jobs to foreigners, many feel as though some of that pie has been given to the strangers/aliens in the house and not the natural born children. Donald Trump won many votes by promising restoration.

Well today is a new day. It is still a day of great harvest. God sent Jesus to give us an abundant life, he did not specify nationalities, only if you be born again. If you be born again, a new creation in Christ Jesus. If ye be transformed by the renewing of your mind, God the Father promises many blessings. The fruits of the spirit….. you can't get them if you don't have the spirit of Christ or if you are ashamed of the spirit of Christ. You are fruitful when you inhabit a land, till the land, work the land, same principle with Jesus, you get His spirit, His anointing, when you are willing to put down your old self, the person with the bad habits, the person with the bad blood, the envy, the jealousy, the ego, the pride the lies, the overindulgence in processed foods, the lack of discipline.. those are the fruits of Satan's spirit, fruits of the flesh.

Galatians 5 states, "Stand fast therefore in the liberty

wherewith Christ hath made us free, and be not entangled again with the yoke of bondage. For we through the Spirit wait for the hope of righteousness by faith. For all the law is fulfilled in one word, even in this; Thou shalt love thy neighbour as thyself. But if ye bite and devour one another, take heed that ye be not consumed one of another. This I say then, Walk in the Spirit, and ye shall not fulfil the lust of the flesh.

For the flesh lusteth against the Spirit, and the Spirit against the flesh: and these are contrary the one to the other: so that ye cannot do the things that ye would."

If you want a harvest, if you want to pick up prosperity, righteous living, a holy life, joy, peace, it will not manifest without some long suffering, patience, kindness, humility. If you want to be prosperous and lack no good thing from the Father, plant seeds of faith.

If you are a farmer you would plant corn, tomatoes, sweet potatoes, grain, barley, green peas and more. You would have cows, goats, cattle, chickens and have a well on your land. You would want of nothing, you would live prosperously off the land.

If you are not a farmer, have no land, live in urban America or suburbia, have no chickens, no cows, no green leafy vegetables growing in your back yard, then you put your money in a bank. You put your trust in that bank and in the government to safeguard your money. But what if a time comes when the government falls short, and we see that happening right now... what about if the banks crash? Where would that leave you? There are many Christians who get public assistance, social security benefits....

What will happen to you if and when the American government fails or falls? Rome fell. And it was known as the world's greatest superpower for 500 years Rome was ruling….. Different factors caused Rome to fall, invasions, much like Isis, political corruption, moral decay of society, climate changes, natural disasters…. Same as what's going on here in America.

My husband, has been a banker for many many years, having been the branch manager at many of the nation's banks, wrote about his prediction of the fall of the banking system in his thesis. What if the banks fail?

What is your plan? Are you going to continually put your trust in man the government, the banks? The Lord is calling on the nations to repent and turn from ungodly ways and to put him first. Most are not listening, but here me today, the bridegroom is coming back to reclaim his church. In what condition will he find the church and the Christians?

Will your trust be in money, the government and the banks? Or will you be trusting in the coming Messiah, Yeshua, the lion of Judah, the Lamb of God, the only one able to break the seven seals?

This is a time to return to the Lord. This is a time to get ready for come what may. If you are not ready you may not be part of that number. There will be all sorts of lying prophets, telling you their messages and not God's. (Jeremiah 23:16 and verse 23). This is a time to turn away from bad habits and live a holy and righteous life. When the bank and government fails, you will be required to take the mark of the beast in order to buy or sell. (Revelation 13:16) "And the second beast required all people small and great, rich and poor, free and slave, to receive a mark on their right hand or on their forehead, <u>so that no one could buy or sell unless he had the</u> mark <u>the name of the beast or the number</u>

of its name."

What will you do then, if all your money and all your livelihood and everything you have is tied up in banks, governments? You may be forced to take the mark of the beast. (Revelation 14: 9) And a third angel followed them, calling in a loud voice, "If anyone worships the beast and its image, and receives its mark on his forehead or hand, he too will drink the wine of God's anger, poured undiluted into the cup of His wrath. And he will be tormented in fire and brimstone in the presence of the holy angels and of the Lamb. And the smoke of their torment will rise forever and ever. Day and night there will be no rest for those who worship the beast and its image, or for anyone who receives the mark of its name." Here is a call for the endurance of the saints who keep the commandments of God and the faith of Jesus. God send me today to tell you prepare yourself for war, learn to live without having to buy or sell, plant a garden, store up bottled water, preserve fruits and vegetables, turn your dependence towards the Lord.

13

Blood Red Tomatoes

With so many things going on around us in our personal lives, sometimes it seems that God has forgotten us. He has not. Your case is before the throne and in due season you will reap if you don't cut down the tree before its time and abandon the task or your assignment.

Watch what you sow. Please say it out loud. "Watch

what you sow." If you plant tomatoes, you will expect tomatoes. You won't plant beans and expect tomatoes. What are you sowing in your own life and how many are you sowing? If you plant one tomato seed, it might not even grow so don't expect a million tomatoes as a harvest. The harvest is relevant to how much you sow. The amount of effort influences and determines progress and success. Tomatoes take about 50 days from the day you plant it till you get that first ripe juicy vitamin C packed tomato. Poor soil, lack of nutrients and lack of water, or too much water, slows down the growth of a tomato plant and may even cause it to die.

Your life is similar to a tomato. If you plant goodness into your life, if you don't tell lies, if you nourish your body well, give it enough water, feed it spiritually by researching and reading the bible every day, by eating healthy foods, not too much indigestible meat, more legumes, and whole grains, green leafy vegetables,... you too will produce good fruit. You will live prosperous lives.

"Beloved, Above all things, I wish that thou mayest prosper and be in good health even as your soul prospers," (3 John 1-2)

Instead, many of us plant cigarette smoke, and excessive alcohol into our bodies and not enough water and we expect to live wholesome happy healthy lives. You get what you plant. Rich fruit, healthy fruit does not grow in toxic conditions. If you want happy, healthy, prosperous lives, you have to watch what you sow. You can stop and start planting goodness into your body and reap a good life.

If you plant lies, your life will be constantly in strife and confusion and problems will follow you. You will not reap a good harvest or life.

It takes the body about 90 days to completely change our blood. New habits can be born in those ninety days. Take three months and transform your life and your health.

That takes faith and patience. You have to want it. How bad do you want it? A good sweet life. It's yours for the taking, Jesus died to set you free from sins and to bring you into a covenant relationship with God the father. It's your inheritance.

So often we allow the enemy to steal our joy. Don't abandon your post because it's rough, start a new regimen, get a new strategy and stick to it. God is looking for soldiers, he is looking for the elite.

We have to get ourselves together for this assignment so we can lead others to salvation before the day of the

Lord.

Are you one of his elite men—the special forces… the ones tried and tested? Are you one of Jesus' trusted friends? Are you going to serve him no matter what? Are you getting ready to serve? Or are you still sowing junk into your life and hoping to manifest ripe fresh anointed fruit? Who are you? What are you made of? When the going gets tough do you run and hide or do you stand and fight? God needs some generals and solders who can take a beating… and still stand… Your faith and your patience go hand in hand… Proverbs 3:5, "Trust in the LORD with all your heart and lean not on your own understanding; in all your ways submit to him, and he will make your paths straight… Look unto the hills from whence coming your help… change your ways…seek the Lord while he may be found… repent change your ways, (your diet) and He will abundantly pardon and give you a new life. Isaiah 55:6

14

Becoming a Millionaire

Money is not everything. Money is just paper. True wealth to me is not having to worry about money, it's having time and good health to enjoy life, helping others become prosperous and spending time with people we love. We must have the means to support ourselves and not spend considerable time obsessing about paper. So examine why you want to make that first million. What would you do with it? Is it to help others or is that you would like to hoard money? Becoming a millionaire does not make you happy. It may make you feel more comfortable, you don't have to worry about your bills so much. You would have other things to worry about though. Like keeping the millions and multiplying them wisely so you don't end up penniless again.

Remember that when you pursue doing the right things, at the right time with and for the right people, all good things will come to you. (Matt 6:33: NLT: Seek the Kingdom of God above all else, and live righteously, and he will give you everything you need.) The richest people are people who have solved a need for others. They have helped millions of people do something easier and faster or they may have a product or service that is extraordinarily convenient (helpful).

If you helped ten thousand people and they paid you $100 each, you would be a millionaire. Or if you met a need of 100,000 people who paid you just $10 each, you just made 1 million dollars. Now if you helped one million people with your book or product or app, you would be a multi-millionaire.

It is better to focus on helping others then than making the millions. Again we ask the question, what can you take to the market that people need or that would make their lives easier and happier?

To answer that question start with what are you good at. Do you have a talent or skill that is remarkable? Next step is to harness that talent, gift or skill and fine tune it. Improve it, research and develop it. Check out your competitors. What makes them successful? How did they get a start? It's also important to get a mentor. When you find a mentor, try to meet them if you can, spend some time with them, do they have seminars or workshops? If so, sign up for one. Buy their products, use their services, see how they packaged it, learn from them. Don't copy them, but learn from the way they do things. You are unique and that uniqueness is what will make you a success at what you do. Make your product or service a great one. Quality is important, learn from all your past efforts and develop a winning product. Pay attention to how your product or service makes people feel. Make sure your customer service is great too.

It's important to check yourself. (Before you wreck yourself.) How are you doing in the market place? How many people are using your products or services and what are they saying about it and about you? Do you have any reviews? Reviews are great especially when you are selling on Amazon. They drive sales. Even if you have to give the product away for free, as free downloads for a specified time, you can use that promotion to get reviews. Keep checking to see how many you are selling, or how many reviews you are getting. If you stay on top of your progress you will be able to build on it, so pay keen attention.

Establish a routine for reaching your goals. For example, you would have to sell $3000 worth of product each day to reach one million in one year. So you have to figure out how many things that has to be to reach that goal. Then you have to do whatever it takes to reach that goal. Everything is possible when you have God on your side. Get a marketing strategy that could help you sell that amount each day. You can sell some on Amazon, by opening an Amazon store. Let's say the item you are selling is a DVD or a book priced at $15 each. Your goal then is to sell 200 DVDs or books each day. Break it down to selling some on your website each day by driving traffic to your website each day. You can do this by daily posting to Facebook and Instagram, some of the benefits people can get from your DVD or book. Track your progress to see how many you sell each day. Keep at trying to help people with your product. Let trying to help people be your focus. Focus on the benefits that they can get. Keep improving your product so they can see and feel the benefits. Word of mouth will spread about how great your product is. Get as many influencers to spread the word about your products. Give them your product as a gift and they will tell people about it.

Advertising is always helpful, though not always cheap. You can generate organic page views if you are diligent at posting and if you are posting interesting and helpful things. Push benefit and how your product will make people feel, rather than hard selling, which will turn people off. On Amazon, you can get increased presence by being on the Amazon chat rooms. Social media has paid platforms for advertising that are inexpensive. Your social media posts must be structured to meet your goals. Pay attention to what works well and what does not work. Repeat what works consistently and diligently follow your strategy to meet your financial goals.

Focus on your marketing efforts persistently. Make YouTube videos to promote your work. Interview people who your product has helped and post those every day. These people should be influencers or even ordinary people. There are other forms of advertising you can employ if you have coupons. Groupon is good when you have a service or health food product. So are direct marketing flyers that you can send to the zip codes you would like to target.

Constantly think of things and services that are unusual

that would help people out. Immigrants often are nostalgic about their country. What services can you provide them that would make them happier? How about dirt? An Irish couple made their first million by selling Irish dirt to homesick immigrants. They gardened with it or threw it on caskets of loved ones buried outside of their birthplace.

Some ministers can sell sermons online to other ministers who may be sick and need a good sermon for the congregation.

Think of something you can invent each day. Write it down and in a couple months you will have a book of "quacky" inventions. Sell it as a physical book or eBook. Or put it on Quirky.com, if they produce your invention you can make that first million. That might make you millions but you will have helped many who don't have as many ideas as you do. It's all about helping people.

That's how you can make millions of dollars. By helping millions of people.

Your marketing strategy to let the millions of people know about your help must be tight. Other sources of publicity and exposure include crowdsourcing. Indiegogo.com, generosity.com are some to try. Don't forget sites like Etsy and Ebay to sell your product. Combine all the above and you will be on your way to selling more than 200 per day of your unique product.

Check out these wacky ideas that netted close to $1 million dollars for its inventors, who were courageous enough to execute their ideas.

1. The Pet Rock netted close to $15 million in nine months. It's a rock sold on a bed of hay that came in a nice box. Hassle free pet!

2. The iFart App sold close to $400000 in downloads. You get to choose from 26 different types of fart sounds and allows users to record-a-fart.

3. The Slinky toy was created in 1945 and has netted billions in sales. It all started when an engineer dropped a spring tension and saw it slink across the room.

4. The Snuggie is a robe blanket for two... sold millions.

5. Beanie Babies raked in $700 million in one year.

15

How to Make Millions by Faith

As I was walking to the supermarket to buy food for our weekly Sunday morning prayer breakfast, a car sped past with the lyrics to a Jay Z song, saying I made more people millions than the Lotto... this one made millions, I made millions, Kanye made millions....

Maybe you too are thinking, how can I make millions? Must I sell drugs and/or be able to spit out lyrics and a sweet beat like Jay Z in order to live the abundant life?

Here are some steps to manifest your millions while living a Christ centered and Christ filled life.

1. Put God first and all the things you desire will be added to your life. Volunteer at an organization serving the Lord. When you do this you align yourself in God's line of vision to receive his mercy, his grace and his favor.
2. Each day think of a million dollar idea that will benefit the world, that will make the world a better place. Develop, patent, run with some of these ideas and they have the potential to make millions of dollars for you.
3. Step out of your comfort zone for the Lord. Would you evangelize on the street for Him? Would you get up early and bring yourself before Him to praise Him and show Him your

love for the sacrifice of his only son Jesus, whose blood was shed on the cross for us?

4. Have the courage to live your truth. Live in truth. Whatever is hidden shall be brought to light anyway. Have the courage to change things about you that you know that the Lord does not approve of. John 10:10 says that Satan comes to steal rob and destroy YOU, but that Jesus came so you can have life more abundantly.

5. Step out on faith and develop your ideas, think of inventions you can invent, books you can write, a business you can start and start it. Don't wait until things are right, make a start, step out on faith, manifest your desires, unleash your potential, God will meet you halfway and open many doors for you. Be focused in

manifesting one thing at a time. Establish one good idea or thing and then move on to the next, growing as you go. But have something to show for your labor. It is called a body of work.

6. Remember to put God first. Deuteronomy 8:18 Remember the Lord thy God, for it is He that gives you power to get wealth. Don't chase after money, chase after doing good work for the Lord.

7. Know that you can do all things through Christ who strengthens you. (Philippians 4:13.) Do not be afraid to step out in faith and manifest your dreams.

8. Knock on some doors and command them to open in Jesus name. Seek and you will find. Go out and ask for what you want. Keep knocking till you get what you want. Get organized. Get

prepared for victory. Know how you will spend your blessed money. Make a plan, have a vision and see where you want to go, map it out and execute your plan.

9. Believe in supernatural miracles. God is Able to do the impossible. He can change situations. Where it looks like a NO, God can change it into a YES. For example, you might think to yourself, there is no possible way I can get a house... I don't have the income, the credit, nor the money. But God is an awesome God, He can make a way and a program just for you. Believe in Him.

10. Stop being convoluted, bitter, burdened down with sin, surrender all of that at the foot of the cross. You know how some people can't see

clearly because of the big mole in their eyes? Ask God to remove it and start you off fresh.

11. Give, Give, Give; Pray, Pray, Pray and Fast, Fast, Fast. The more you give the more you will be blessed. Donation, tithes and offerings will bless your income stream.

God is able, my friend. He will see you through. He loves a "reacher." Without faith it is impossible to please Him. Here's to a more abundant life. Believe God for it and reach for it. Don't stop until you are living the life you desire.

16

Plan for Prosperity

There is a prosperity plan and system for prosperity in the bible. However if we don't study the master's word, we will never learn the plan. When we realize that God wants us to plan for prosperity through using faith, it changes our perspective and drives tangible results. We start preparing for success and preparing for opportunities. We become more alert, less we miss any blessing that God is sending our way.

The first step in planning for the increase is to put our flesh in subjection to the will of God. In other words, we just can't do whatever our flesh dictates to our mind or feels like doing. We have to control ourselves and control our thoughts and action. (Romans 8: 5-8) Some people often 'flip' and commit atrocious deeds, like violence against another, bank robbery or even murder. When they say they 'flipped', they mean that they were not in control of their body, they let emotions control their minds and body. Many of those people go to jail for those actions.

Discipline begins with our thoughts. We have power to control our thoughts. Thoughts turn into action if we act on them, so we must control our thoughts and emotions. Discipline is key to prosperity. We can't prosper and our families can't prosper if we are locked up. Satan wants us to flip, so that they can lock us up, thereby destroying families.

Proper planning for opportunity is very necessary. How can you get the blessings if you are not prepared? If you are thirsty and praying for rain, you should get a cup or vessel to store the rainwater when it falls. The widow of Zarephath had to go get containers to store the overflow of oil and flour, after she gave to the prophet Elijah. (1 Kings 17)

In these times you prepare for financial blessings by preparing bank accounts, by researching investments and getting the appropriate training or licenses to manage and multiply the blessings. If you would like to move out of your old apartment and into a bigger house, you start preparing for this blessing by looking for a new house. Get a realtor or look in the newspapers for real estate that suit your needs. Don't let the fact that you may not have money now stop you. You are readying yourself for the blessing, so that when the money comes, you will be ready.

If you are praying for a baby, get a baby's room ready. God respects faith and He makes a way for the faithful ones. The plans of the diligent profit but laziness leads to poverty. Slow minded, lazy people don't make plans because it requires too much effort to plan and execute plans, so instead, they follow other people's plans and constantly ask for direction. Diligent people are always looking for opportunity. They are the ones you see taking calculated business risks, selling things, making things to sell, doing trade, writing books, putting on events, starting several businesses. They will make it not only because they are always striving and seeking diligently for ways to prosper, but because of the tremendous effort they put in. God makes a way for the diligent.

Even if you feel tired and worn out, keep putting that effort in. It is difficult to start again when you have been beat down so many times in the past. When you have failed over and over again. When this is perhaps your third marriage and it's not going so good either. When you get that bad diagnosis from the doctor that you have a disease that is terminal or unknown. These things are scary, unknown territory. That's not the time to worry and be afraid, that's the time to mount up a defense, a plan of action. Worrying, fear and stress lead to death. People don't seem to know how precious human life is. A blow to your system, be it mental system, emotional system, physical system or spiritual system can kill us if we are not resilient or even alert enough to withstand the attack. The enemy gets happy when they see us staying down for the count. However they didn't count on that ace up your sleeve. That angel investor, that backer, that silent partner, that best friend of yours, the one with the unmatched healing supernatural power. Some call him Yeshua, some call him Jesus. He is awesome. With Him as a friend you can do all things.

When you are planning for prosperity, be prepared to work hard to dig a deep foundation. Depending on your team, you may be building a foundation for years. Your reputation is a great foundation to build. So is your credit. Build up your credit, so as to prepare for the opportunities coming your way. When I was buying that first home, the first thing that I did is that I started working on my credit, it took many months, but I used discipline and called all my creditors, made agreements and paid off my debt so my credit could be good enough to get a house. This requires focus, planning and effort. I have noted that many people put in .5 percent effort and they always want to reap 100 percent. That's not how life works, except for gambling which should not be our plan for prosperity. Anything you desire in life, you can get depending on the amount of effort you put in. If you were a farmer and could only afford to plan twenty-five tomato seeds, you don't expect millions of tomatoes. So to get millions you have to put tremendous effort into planning and planting the right amount of seeds to equal that kind of harvest.

Without realizing it, people make plans to destroy themselves. We plan for most sin. Some buy unhealthy food and liquor to watch pornography. Some buy liquor and drugs to seduce a man or woman, some plan ways to get revenge. We sometimes plan not to go to church. So we make plans for everything. We plan for vacations, some save money in a jar or holiday club for that vacation and would not deliberately miss the plane after we have bought tickets. Likewise, we must plan for prosperity and follow through. We plan for everything else we desire in life, so we must make a plan if we would like to acquire wealth, good health and prosperity. Do you have a valid plan for prosperity or is it just a wish? After you have made a realistic plan for long term prosperity, don't miss the plane. Since this is a long term plan, it requires annual inspection and revision. If your goal is to save $12,000 yearly by putting aside $1000 each month, then in December or after the twelve month period, pay attention to what you will do with that $12,000. Consider saving that amount each year. Look into purchasing annuities that have higher interest rates. Some online banks have greater interest rates than brick and mortar banks since they may only have one headquarters instead of multiple branches.

Those savings are passed on to the consumer. Research American Express bank and Ally Bank to name a couple.

We need discipline to become wealthy, healthy and prosperous. We need discipline to deny our flesh the unhealthy cheeseburger with white bread and imitation cheese. We need discipline to get some exercise each day. We need discipline to drink eight glasses of water each day. We need discipline to not over indulge in alcohol, cigarettes, drugs, desserts, food, worry, sinful thoughts and deeds, sex, spending, shopping, talking and so on. Too much of anything is unhealthy. With discipline, we need persistence and repetition. Keep your eyes on the prize and keep saving until you reach your goals.

In order to go from poverty to prosperity and by poverty I mean poor health, poor lifestyle, living paycheck to paycheck and being broke financially; we must be transformed by the renewing of our mind. (Romans 12:2) Start reading different types of books, romance novels might have to make way for non-fiction books that can teach you something or show you a different perspective. You will need to hang out with a different bunch of people. You need a mind, body and soul makeover. If the church you're in is stagnant, visit other churches, hear from other preachers, become more spiritually developed. If you don't go to church, start going. It's fun and your faith will be developed. Again, we need to put effort into transforming. Sin and bad lifestyle choices mess up our plans for prosperity. Sometimes we try to take a shortcut, but that messes us up too and can lead to death.

This week I have seen how fragile the human being is. I have seen people break down and die because of spiritual blows to their system and constant attacks to their emotional system, this weakened their physical body so much that they could not fight and their body could not defend itself against any virus or disease. We must strengthen up ourselves and do what is right in God's sight. We are to take off the old coat before putting on the new coat. We cannot wear them both simultaneously. We must let go of the old us before we become brand new prosperous people. We cannot think and do the same old things and expect new results. Change is necessary and it takes discipline, keen focus and effort.

These seven revelations will bring blessings into your life:

1. Knowing what your purpose is (1 Peter 2:9) When you know your purpose, you have a destination in your mind and you are able to navigate straight to it without wasting precious

time and without allowing Satan to distract, deter, deny and destroy you.

2. Learning what our gifts are and letting go and letting God's healing powers to regenerate and heal us as they restore us. "By His stripes you are healed, he died not only for our sins but he took our illnesses and ailments to the cross with him. (Isaiah 53:5)

3. Power to speak blessings into lives and power to manifest blessings. (Proverbs 18:20-21) "Death and life *are* in the power of the tongue: and they that love it shall eat the fruit thereof." Learning to speak blessings instead of curses attracts blessings. Speak positive things into your life and think of positive things rather than negative things and see your thoughts materialize. Put positive action behind positive

words and see things happen for you that you've only dreamed of. Write down what you want to attract and attract into the life the kind of people, friends and even spouse that you desire to be close to.

4. As you get closer to God by studying His word (bible) your self-esteem will increase. As you begin to feel better about yourself and the new creation that you are now become, it will cause holy boldness to be birthed in you. This boldness will allow you to do and start great things, businesses, write books and do things that you thought you couldn't do. You will now be able to manifest a new reality, a new life for yourself.

5. Discernment for God to direct your path. God has plans to prosper you and give you life, hope

and a future. Despite your past God will make a way for you and open doors for you that no one can shut.

6. Favor of God will be on you. As you continue to study and obey God's word and live a life pleasing to God, He will give you increased favor. Just like God gave Nehemiah favor with King Artaxerxes, He will give you favor with powerful people. When I started publishing the community empowerment magazine, although I was an independent publisher, a small local one woman show, God gave me favor to meet and greet President Obama and the First Lady several times. I could not have opened that door by myself, I did not have the money or the connections to do so. It was simply God. God will cause you to be in the right place at the

right time to meet the right people to take you to the next stages in your journey. Be ready for the opportunities, like Nehemiah was when he got an audience with the king. Know what you want and where you would like to go.

7. Listen carefully for God's guidance. God will speak to your spirit if you tune in to His frequency. His frequency is not loud like the rest of the world. It is a small still voice. It is often the voice of reason, but sometimes you may be led to do unusual things. Obedience is key here to opening up financial blessings. When you obey God, He rewards you. In Hebrews, the book of faith, one of my favorite passages is the one that tells us that God is a rewarder of those who diligently seek Him. (Hebrews 11:6) When you seek someone out, it

is to follow them, to be with them. You don't seek out people to then go the opposite or do the opposite of what they ask you.

If you follow these spiritual guidelines, you will be financially blessed and favored in all areas of your life. Remember that, "Whoever pursues righteousness and love finds life, prosperity and honor." (Proverbs 21:21)

17

Anointed to Lead

Does anyone need strength to continue on? Does anyone feel weak and tired like you're holding on by a string? You have a choice? You can continue to feel this way or you can choose to strengthen up in the Lord. It is time to choose to feel joy because the joy of the Lord is your strength... Habakkuk 3:17

Happiness and joy is a choice. If one strengthens you

and the other weakens you with worry, why not choose the one that offers you strength. It's like taking a drink: One weakens you, tires you and the other refreshes you, and strengthens you. Choose joy!!!

"The Lord is my strength and my shield, my heart trusted in Him and I am helped, therefore my heart greatly rejoices." Psalm 28:7

It is important to memorize some verses to speak strength and joy into our lives in those trying times and weak moments:

The enemy fears this power to speak blessings into your own lives. Try memorizing the following psalm in times of uncertainty and trouble.

"The LORD is my light and my salvation; whom shall I fear? The LORD is the strength of my life; of whom shall I be afraid?

² When the wicked, even mine enemies and my foes, came upon me to eat up my flesh, they stumbled and fell.

³ Though an host should encamp against me, my heart shall not fear: though war should rise against me, in this will I be confident.

⁴ One thing have I desired of the LORD, that will I seek after; that I may dwell in the house of the LORD all the days of my life, to behold the beauty of the LORD, and to enquire in his temple.

⁵ For in the time of trouble he shall hide me in his pavilion: in the secret of his tabernacle shall he hide me; he shall set me up upon a rock.

⁶ And now shall mine head be lifted up above mine enemies round about me: therefore will I offer in his

tabernacle sacrifices of joy; I will sing, yea, I will sing praises unto the LORD." (Psalm 27)

Amen... Hallelujah.. What a mighty God we serve....

Beloved, you have what it takes, right now.

Your ideas, your skills, your experiences make you very special, set apart, unique.

Be confident in your abilities. Do not dwell on what you lack, give thanks for all that you have.. The joy of the Lord is your strength.

If you didn't know the Lord, I would expect you to be stressed out, afraid, living in fear of the enemy, he is a thief after all, a murderer and he is looking for people to tear up. He is looking for lives to destroy. He is looking for minds to confuse, people to tempt, people to indulge in their flesh, people to overdose, people to have abortions, people to do drugs, people to turn out into homosexuals and lesbians... all to set you back and keep you from living an abundance life. He hates you, blinds you by sin, lies to you, fools you, all to keep you poor and sick or rich and immoral.

Why not choose the Lord and his son Jesus, born of Mother Mary and conceived by the Holy Spirit? He is a miracle worker, He is a deliverer, He is a rescuer, He is the Lamb of God, He is the lion of Judah, He is worthy of our trust and our praise. He is our savior. He shed His blood so we can be freed from all the chains, lies and ropes of deception that Satan has tied up our feet and minds in. Jesus gives us the power to break free of every chain. Hallelujah!!!

God wants you to know today that you are rich. Heirs and heiress, you are his children and God wants to remind you above all things to prosper, and to be in great health, even as your soul prospers. {3 John 1-2}

Poverty is mental but manifests a physical condition. It is the absence of ideas, imagination, determination and faith. You can break the chain of poverty by not being afraid to act on your ideas, by knowing that your father is God and that you can do all things through Christ.

God did not create the earth with money. He spoke it into existence. You have the same power. Today we are going to speak into existence what we desire out of life. We are then going to write it down. Write down the vision.

Don't worry about not having money. Make sure you have accepted Jesus into your life as your personal savior. Then you will be free and rich. I can do all things through Christ... you have to accept Christ for that to statement to work.

Please find a quiet place to speak to the Almighty One. Your creator, your rich Dad. Show him the vision and ask Him what He thinks. Go on your knees, it will go better for you and is a sign of respect. Do not get up until you have quieted your thoughts to be on the same frequency of God and have received clarification, confirmation, ideas, a picture in your mind... wait for God to answer you before you get up.

Then go start your vision. Don't be afraid. Not having money should not slow you down, it has never stopped me. I faked it until I made it. I simply keep acting and believing that great wealth would overtake me, that one of my ideas or businesses would take off. My eggs are not in one basket, one should have a diversified portfolio like the widow of Zarephath, she had multiple barrels that filled up with oil.

Use what you have. Joel 3:10 says make a sword out of

your plowshare and turn your pruning scissors into spears and let the weak say, "I am a mighty warrior/solder. I am strong!" Fake it until you make it.

When you use your faith, it attracts blessings and favors into your life. Get excited by your birthright! Get excited over your inheritance. Don't let Satan just waltz in and steal it from you... Turn whatever you have into a spear and a sword and fight him. Then go into the enemy's camp and take back what he stole from you..... The Lord is your light and salvation whom shall you fear! He is the strength of your life. You are freed from Satan's chains, depression and his stronghold. Break free today..... Use the joy of the Lord to be strong.

I am praying for your strength I pray that you will break free. I pray that you will rise, I pray that you conquer the demon or demons that Satan sent to defeat you. I pray that every chain will fall off and be set fire to right now in Jesus name. I bind every demon that was sent to devour your blessings, to tamper with you, to mess up your mind, to kill and destroy you, to keep you broke, you are His child, an heiress, an heir of the Most High, you are royalty. Put on the full armor and fight for the kingdom.

"I have anointed you to go and teach the glad tidings to the poor"." (Isaiah 61v 1)

18

Paralysis

Fear is defined in the dictionary as a feeling induced by perceived danger or threat, which causes a change in metabolic and organ functions and ultimately a <u>change in behavior</u>, such as fleeing, hiding, or <u>freezing</u> from perceived traumatic events. Fear in human beings may occur in response to a specific stimulus occurring in the present, or in anticipation or expectation of a future threat perceived as a risk to body or life. The fear response arises from the perception of danger leading to confrontation with or escape from/avoiding the threat (also known as the fight-or-flight response), which in extreme cases of fear (horror and terror) can be a freeze response or **paralysis**.

Fear can cause people to stop moving, stop striving, stop thinking or it can cause them to run and hide. Men in particular have a fear of not being able to provide. I spoke to several men and that is their number one fear. This fear actually paralyses some men into inaction. They will see their wives and children go to bed hungry or go without necessities and they will do nothing. Their wives think they are lazy and inadequate, but they are not. They are paralyzed by fear. They fear their wives will divorce them and take away their children, because what kind of man is not able to take care of his family?

This bothers the male who is not able to hunt and bring in provisions via income. It bothers them to the point where they can become stagnant and thereby fulfil their fears. These types of fears most often come from divorce, loss of a job or loss of a loved one, imprisonment and/or illness.

This is a good time to press the reset button of our minds and to renew our thinking. No matter how bad things get, we can get an angel backer, an angel investor, a champion, a best friend at our side. His name is Jesus, He is the son of God and the bible says, "Who is it that can overcome the world? He that believes that Jesus is the son of God." (1 John 5:5)

When you believe that and act on this belief you can do all things through Jesus Christ. That is Jesus' purpose. His name Yeshua is Hebrew for rescuer. Christ stems from the Greek word Christos which means anointed, which means made holy by oil, water and/or the Holy Spirit.

Today we see so many inadequate people, lost people, people suffering and they all seem to believe that their misery comes from being broke financially. Being broke spiritually causes broke finances. If you believe yourself wealthy you will be wealthy. I always knew I would be wealthy. I chose to believe that because we can choose what to believe and that shapes our destiny.

I have seen rich people live miserable lives because they are spiritually broken. Many of them have been corrupted by their love of money, their greed and their disregard for God. They are spiritually dense and they believe in the power of money more than the power of God. Yet they believe they have power because they have money or position and so they bumble around importantly living meaningless and sinful lives that lead to destruction.

If we are not serving God then we are serving Satan, there are two masters, one good and the other evil. Choose today who you will serve. Eternity is a long time. Our children and grandchildren inherit our ways, our wealth or debt, our health (eating habits), our folly and also our sins. What will your legacy be?

If we allow fear to paralyze us we remain frozen for some time. It is a bad time for the people around you. You will not be producing, your thinking will be off. It's like you're in a standing, walking comatose state. Let this wake you up: you are more than a conqueror. You can go out there and do anything you put your mind and heart to. Note that I said "go out there." Although you feel like staying inside and hiding, go out there. Pray and ask God to give you ideas and a plan, then you dress for success and go out there with the Lord and do something. Don't stop doing that. By being consistent, each day you will be building the life you want to live and each day you will be building the legacy you will be leaving behind. Every single day matters. A good way out of the paralysis caused by fear is to go back to school and reinvent yourself by starting a new career or by getting qualifications and certifications that can enable you to provide forever. Choose the most in demand careers and businesses so that you won't have to worry about the fear of not providing becoming a reality. A rolling stone gathers no moss. You will waste time when you stand paralyzed by fear, your mind panicking but your body refusing to move, spring that body into action and run to the nearest school so you can register for classes. There are short courses you can take that will advance your career. If you love to cook and have skills in the kitchen, take a food handlers' permit course and research culinary schools.

Some women worry about getting married a little too much. Relax buttercups! There is absolutely someone out there for you. You don't have to go looking for him either, he is searching for you. You do have to get your mind ready for him when he comes, personal development courses, classes, workshops, seminars, events and keep busy working, travelling, living a full and sin free life. He will find you quicker if you follow the above steps. If you stay inside and do nothing but eat, he won't find you and if by chance he knocks on your door, you don't want to be too overweight. The more you do, the more calories you will burn. Walking up and down the stairs to the various classes, meetings or seminars helps you burn calories and keeps your mind fit as well. So get out there and do some interesting things. There's Zumba, you make friends there, you may go out with these friends to a restaurant and sitting across the room at the bar, is the man of your dreams staring straight at you. Smile at him dead in his eyes for 15 seconds and then look away.

I met my husband at the bank. He was the new manager and I was the lady with the business account. I went there to put some of my community magazines in his branch. He asked me what the magazine was about and if I had an account there. We talked and I found out that he was in the middle of a divorce. Some months later I happened to be travelling to the mountains with my daughter and foster daughter and I happened to call him. Turned out he lived in the mountains where I was heading. He invited us over. The rest is history. We were married three years later.

Some men and women have a fear of choosing the right man or woman to marry. This fear can paralyze them into inaction and they delay getting married and living prosperous healthy whole lives. Marriage is honorable and Satan absolutely hates marriage and family. He prefers his victims to be alone when he comes to kill, steal and destroy. If there are two his chances are not as certain because one will warn the other. "Watch out sweetie, I see the enemy coming to attack you." It's easier for him to pick on you if you are single. It's easier for him to steal your blessings if you are single. It's easier for him to entice you into sin if you are lonely and single. When you get married it makes him angry. Now you have a better chance of pleasing God, now you are going to attempt to raise strong healthy kids, now you have stability, now you have a partner to warn you when he is about to strike you out, now you have a partner to encourage you, to love you, to feed you and to protect you. Now you have a partner to pay half the bills maybe, you don't have to kill yourself working three jobs to put food on the table. Now you have a companion to go out with, so you don't have to sit at the movies by yourself or eat dinner by yourself or covet another man or woman's spouse. Now you have your own. A partner to build wealth with. A partner to open a join account with and save your money. A partner to go on vacation with, a partner to run your ideas by and see what he or she thinks. Marriage can allow you to live an abundant life. Jesus came to give us an abundant life and what happened to Him? They killed him. Satan does not want you to have an abundant and prosperous life. So he will try to kill your marriage just like they killed Jesus. Now you see where I am going with this, try to allow your marriage to be all the good things mentioned above. Be that encouraging spouse. Put some effort and consistence into listening to your spouse and treating them with kindness. Try to understand what your spouse is feeling and put some serious effort into meetings those needs. It's very simple. Husbands number one need is for intimacy, they like being loved on, kissed and to feel like they are the best thing ever happened to you. Wives number one need is for security. We like to feel taken care of. We don't want to tell you what to do, when to do it and how to do it. We really don't. We love a man who knows how to take charge and get things done, like Nehemiah. When husbands meet that number one need of wives, we feel free to give them all the intimacy they can handle.

A stalemate is when husbands are not getting intimacy because wives are not getting security. Husbands that need to be told how and when to do everything are not being productive. Not only does the woman have to bring in the bacon, she has now has another child to take care of. No one wants to sleep with a child. We want men who take their gender seriously and go out there and find a way to bring in the bacon, legally. At Christmas time, we want men who either put up the Christmas lights outside the house or volunteer to help put them up without being asked.

Men want wives who they find attractive, (beauty is in the eyes of the beholder) wives that can be productive, can help them save and build wealth while simultaneously raising healthy children. They want wives who meet their need for intimacy in the bedroom. So ladies, don't let the enemy sabotage your marriage by paralyzing you with fear, where you stay at home and get fat not believing that you are worthy of your spouse. Get up and go out there and keep your spouse happy by giving them what they need.

Sometimes the enemy uses illness to separate spouses. Illness can cause poverty since one or two are unable to work. Understand that illness will come from unhealthy eating habits or from accidents. Not drinking water on a daily basis will cause illness later in life. Having a sweet tooth and over-indulging in cakes, candy, soda, white flour, white sugar, pork, shrimp, lobster and more can bring on disease. Have the courage and foresight to change your eating habits so you can live an abundant life. Most diseases that they say are hereditary stem from a long family history of eating unhealthy foods and living unhealthy lifestyles. Do you hate walking, working out or any forms of exercise? Learn to like fun sweaty activity.

This week, I have learnt about two marriages dissolving, one of the couples I married less than three years ago, the other had been married about three years also. In both these marriages I found that prosperity was an issue. Both spouses have a need for prosperity, which is defined as good fortune, successful, flourishing, thriving conditions, especially financially. Although people marry for better or worse, we take a chance that our spouse will not take us to a worse condition because we all want prosperity. When spouses don't see any change for the better, we get nervous and feel that maybe we may have made the wrong decision. The partner that's not doing too well in the relationship, meaning, he or she may not be contributing financially or may be enrolled in a school, that person feels bad that they are not able to contribute. The other spouse feels bad that the burden is on him or her to do everything. So both spouses feel less than happy. Then there is pride, which as you know, goes before a fall. Pride gets in the way of making comprises, concessions. The one that's not contributing reminds the spouse that they married for better and for worse. They don't understand the other spouse's need for a break, a night out perhaps, because they are so caught up in trying to get themselves together financially. So someone outside the marriage fulfills that need for the other spouse, who may now be tempted to leave the marriage that is in the 'worse' state. Many marriages that are caught in the 'worse' state neglect the need for entertainment, for a time out. By the time they figure it out, the moment has passed and the other spouse has moved on mentally. If you are caught up in a relationship like this, call someone else who can talk to your spouse for you, like an aunt or uncle, who can talk some sense into them, by making them to understand how you are feeling. The worse thing is to do nothing, because it will grow and fester and result in irreconcilable differences.

Understand that there is a thief out there looking to rob you of your health, your money and your husband or wife. That means you have to protect these assets. You don't sleep with your doors unlocked, do you? It's the same way you must fiercely guard what you consume. Over consumption will bring obesity then you won't be able to run when the thief comes. You will be paralyzed by fear. Over spending brings lack and when you need money you won't have any, allowing brokenness and divorce into your life. Don't sleep on Satan. He is a mean, slick, thief and he is a liar. He uses fear to paralyze his victims and then he robs them of every joy in their life. You don't have to be a victim anymore, you can be a victor. Walk with Lord Jesus and you will win every time, even when it looks like they won, the tides will turn and you will be the ultimate winner. Don't give up. Get up and go out there and get what is for you and your family. Even if fear had you paralyzed for a moment, a year or a decade, wake up now while there is still time and go about changing the direction that your life is going. You can do it. God did not give you a spirit of fear when He created you. He gave you power and a sound mind. In that sound mind of yours, there is untapped wealth and resources. Pray and access it right now. You are an heir or heiress, you are not a pauper. Jesus died for you to bring you an inheritance of abundant life. Go out there and live that abundant life in Jesus name. Don't stop trying, if you don't give up, you will inherit. Get back up, dust your behind off and get back on that horse. Ride to freedom, ride on to wealth, ride for better health, ride for a new career, ride for your children's future, ride to leave a legacy of prosperity.

19

WISDOM

"The man who fears God will avoid all extremes.

Wisdom make one wise man more powerful than ten rulers in a city." (Ecclesiastes 7:18)

There is not a righteous man on earth who does what is right and never sins. Jesus was the only such man. We strive to live a righteous life, but we are all guilty of sinful thoughts and/or sinful deeds.

"To the ones that please God He gives wisdom, knowledge and happiness, but to the sinner he gives the task of gathering and storing up wealth to hand over to the one who pleases God." Ecclesiastes 2:26

"There is a time and place for everything and a season for every activity under heaven. There is time to die, a time to plant, and a time to uproot, a time to kill and a time to heal, a time to tear down and time to build up, a time to weep and a time to laugh, a time to mourn and a time to laugh, a time to scatter stones and a time to gather them, a time to embrace and a time to refrain, a time to search and a time to give up, a time to keep an a time to throw away, a time to tear and a time to mend, a time to be silent and a time to speak, a time to love and a time to hate, a time for war and time for peace." (Ecclesiastes 3:1)

Timing and favor is everything. We must always strive

to be at the right place at the right time with the right people saying the right words, doing the right things. The wise have eyes in their head but the fool walks in darkness, but yet the same fate can come to both of them.

Whatever you put your strongest efforts to in life will manifest for you. Work hard for the Lord so that He can give you the desires of your heart. That is a secret that many do not understand because they would rather work hard to accomplish their own desires and pleasures. I have found that when you serve the Lord with all your might, He simply blesses you with all you desire. Why worry when you have the favor of God on your life. The more you serve Him, the more you rely on Him, the more you trust Him, the more you pray and worship Him, the more He blesses you. That is why I work feverishly hard in the vineyard, because there is so much to do and so few people to do it. People do not know the secret to success, "Remember the Lord thy God for it is He that gives you power to get wealth," (Deuteronomy 8:18.) God loves the servants that keep busy. If you have workers and servants, do you like the ones who are lazy and always going on an unhealthy smoke or unhealthy food breaks or do you prefer the ones who stay at their post diligently planning ways to increase your territory? Would you like the workers who get sick all the time because of unhealthy lifestyles or would you prefer the ones who eat healthy and try to stay fit so they can serve you better? Would you rather the workers or servants that research and study you to know what you want, they consult with you and then spring into action or would you rather the ones you have to constantly tell what to do? Who would you bless with promotion and wealth? The ones that are mentally lazy, the ones who don't want to think because thinking leads to action or the ones that are mentally alert and efficient, proactive and busy?

The theologians believe that the book of Ecclesiastes was written by the wealthiest, wisest man of the bible era, King Solomon. He should know a thing or two about life, wealth and the pursuit of happiness. He had harems, built impressive gardens, temples, you name it he did it. And he concludes that all of that is meaningless, that the only meaningful thing in life is living a life to please God.

This week my cousin passed away. She was strong and healthy and no one saw it coming. Her husband had just fell off a ladder and died and six months later, here she was in the hospital with a mysterious skin disease, which had her skin literally falling off. She could not lay on her back because her skin would literally stick on the bed. Within a few weeks she was dead. I felt strongly when I visited her alive at the hospital that it was also a spiritual blow and not just physical. She had wronged someone who was seeking revenge by way of witchcraft. I prayed to God to cancel this attempt by the enemy. I remember her telling me about a dream she had had that someone else wanted her bed at her house. I also remember her telling me that she was unable to read her bible at the hospital. She was so afraid, her mind was panicking because of the condition of her skin. And she was confined, paralyzed, to the hospital bed. Human life is very frail, a severe spiritual blow, physical blow, emotional blow can kill us if we are not careful.

My sister called me and said let us go to the hospital and support our cousin's daughter, who was there alone tending to her mother. I dropped my sister off and before I had turned the corner to park the vehicle, she called and said our cousin had died. I parked and went upstairs. Our cousin, lay dead in the hospital room. Her skin was still warm and her spirit was alive and talking. She was worried about going to the Lord. I understood and prayed that the gates of heaven would open for her at God's Kingdom. After much praying, her spirit calmed down and started travelling to the Light of the Lord. I opened her bible which lay at her bedside and I cut on a verse that she had underlined. It was in the book of Ecclesiastes. This was the newly dead's message to us here on earth.

"This *is* an evil among all *things* that are done under the sun, that *there is* one event unto all: yea, also the heart of the sons of men is full of evil, and madness *is* in their heart while they live, and after that *they go* to the dead. For to him that is joined to all the living there is hope:

for a living dog is better than a dead lion.

For the living know that they shall die: but the dead know not anything, neither have they any more a reward; for the memory of them is forgotten.

Also their love, and their hatred, and their envy, is now perished; neither have they any more a portion forever in any*thing* that is done under the sun.

Go your way, eat your bread with joy, and drink your wine with a merry heart; for God now accepts your works.

Let your garments be always white; and let your head lack no ointment.

Live joyfully with the wife whom you love all the days of the life of your vanity, which he has given you under the sun, all the days of your vanity: for that is your portion in this life, and in your labor which you perform under the sun.

Whatsoever your hand finds to do, do it with all your might; for there is no work, nor device, nor knowledge, nor wisdom, in the grave, where you go." (Ecclesiastes 9: 3-10)

20

Promotion

God, in His infinite wisdom, has equipped us with all

the tools we need to live an abundant and prosperous life. The rest is up to us now. If we are slothful, we may just miss the inheritance. If we are lazy, the blessing will go to another who is diligent. Let us then strive for excellence in everything that we do. When we are at work, at school, wherever we go, remember that we are God's servant, and must live a life worthy of the great inheritance that we have.

Instead of pursuing money, let us pursue righteous living and all the desires of our heart shall follow. The love of money is the root of all evil, so let us learn to love God the Father, the Son and the Holy Spirit instead of loving money, which we have to leave behind when we die. Living a meaningful life means living to please God, serving Him and being the best servants to a mighty master. This is the secret to prosperity, pleasing God.

Let us learn from King Solomon, the wisest king that ever lived and probably the wealthiest as well. He found that even with all his wealth, wives, property and position, the only worthwhile thing in life was serving and pleasing God.

Therefore at the top of your list, put prayer. It is

necessary to ask God what He wants of us. We need to humble ourselves and pray more. We need to ask God for direction in our life. As we come to the foot of the throne of the master, we need to surrender our pride and ego and give Him our all. Let us give our best servitude, our best lives so that He will be pleased with us and bless us for a thousand generations.

God absolutely speaks to our spirit, are we listening though? Endeavor to listen more to that voice of the Holy Spirit, pay attention to your instincts, they are there to warn us of danger. Pay attention to the little details. Remember that laziness causes depression. When you don't reach your goals you will become very depressed and your self-esteem falls too. So do your best to follow through. They say that the fortune is in the follow-up and that is true. If you don't follow up, you don't get an opportunity to pick up the check.

People also lose interest in you and whatever you're selling if there is no follow up. So make up your mind that you will be as hard-working as possible and have a strong marketing strategy and business plan that you take to the Lord in prayer. He is after all, your backer.

When you take God as your backer, miracles happen. Obstacles move out of your way. People suddenly change their mind and doors open that no man can shut. The benefits of having the Lord as your backer are tremendous. Your faith determines your salary. Your service determines your increase. Your diligence determines how much you will expand and how long you will be prosperous.

Many people run from the Lord, believing they are not ready to work on this level with the Creator. This is an error of judgement. The longer you run, the longer it will take you to find your way. It is like running from yourself because His spirit lives in you. He is the Creator. Many go around in circles, because they want to do whatever sinful thoughts and actions come to them, then they find themselves in trouble and come back to the Lord. Still others keep going along a dark and slippery path without knowing that they can turn on their inner light and totally see where they are going, so that they can change paths quickly instead of heading for the fall.

After a fall, it's important not to wallow in self-pity but to ask God to show you the way. His grace is sufficient to put you on a better path that will lead to greatness and prosperity and all the desires of your heart.

In the army of the Lord, God allows us to set our own salary through trust and faith. He will supply all your needs. The workers in the God's kingdom are few, there is much work to do and the harvest is great. God is looking for more people that He can trust, train and send out there to work for Him. The pay is limitless, we get bonus blessings, healing plan, protection plan, by faith credit cards, vision plan and these benefits can be transferred or rolled over generation to generation. There is no background check into your past, all you have to do is change your thinking and change your life. It is the best servant job on earth, with room for promotion that's literally out of this world **and** His elite, handpicked, anointed, team are considered royalty. If you apply yourself to finding, working and living your purpose, with God as your backer and boss, you will succeed beyond your wildest dreams. Go for it, don't hold back, give life your best shot and enjoy the ride. God promises that if we keep going, and don't give up or fall back, that He will give us more energy to do more and that He will give us wings, so that we can soar. I love flying and those dreams I always had of flying have been manifested. I invite you to join me in working for the Lord. He will supply all your needs according to His riches and glory.

"Now unto him that is able to do exceeding abundantly above all that we ask or think, according to the power that works in us, unto him *be* glory in the church by Christ Jesus throughout all ages, world without end. Amen. "(Ephesians 3:20)

ABOUT THE AUTHOR

Rev. Dr. Roxanne Simone Lord Marcelle is a pastor, inspirational speaker and author of five books. The Last Castle in Brooklyn, Tapping into Divine Abundance, Get Out of Your Cage, Summer Camp for Young Super Heroes and Financial Freedom by Faith. Her workshops, such as Never Be Broke Again and books help people to break negative patterns and to live abundant lives and make her a captivating and sought after motivational speaker for all age groups.. A visit to www.SimoneLord.org will inspire you as you discover Rev. Lord's "ICAN" Divine Healing Candles, books and videos.

R. Simone Lord Marcelle is also the founder and president of the Southeast Queens Chamber of Commerce. Her corporate background, journalistic and media career has allowed her to meet and greet President Obama, First Lady Michelle Obama and interview many powerful leaders, Pulitzer Prize winners, artists, literary geniuses and thinkers.

Dr. Lord Marcelle has earned honorary doctorate degrees in Humanities and Ministry and also has a Bachelor of Arts degree from Brooklyn College, New York. Dr. Lord is the recipient of numerous awards from the US Senate, Brooklyn Borough President, Mayor of New York, Council of New York and many more.

She is married and is currently completing a doctorate in Naturopathic Medicine and is a certified health care practitioner.

Contact Dr Lord Marcelle by visiting www.SimoneLord.org or email peoplesfirstbaptistchurch@gmail.com Tel: 888-312-2016

Roxanne Simone Lord

www.ingramcontent.com/pod-product-compliance
Lightning Source LLC
Chambersburg PA
CBHW020850090426
42736CB00008B/323